SOCIAL

WORLD

of the

HEBREW

PROPHETS

SOCIAL
WORLD
of the
HEBREW
PROPHETS

VICTOR H. MATTHEWS

HENDRICKSON
PUBLISHERS

Printed in the United States of America

First printing — October 2001

Cover: original art depicting Samuel anointing Saul, by Anna Iamim, Lower Galilee, Israel.

Except where otherwise noted, Scripture quotations are from the New Revised Standard Version of the Bible copyright © 1989 by the Division of Christian Education of the National Council of the Churches of Christ in the United States of America and are used by permission.

Library of Congress Cataloging-in-Publication Data

Matthews, Victor Harold.
    Social world of the Hebrew prophets / Victor H. Matthews.
    Includes bibliographical references and index.
    ISBN 1-56563-417-9 (hardcover : alk. paper)
    1. Bible. O.T. Prophets—Socio-rhetorical criticism.
  2. Palestine—Social life and customs—To 70 A.D. I. Title.
BS1505.2 .M355 2001
224'.06—dc21
                                    2001005668

TABLE OF CONTENTS

Abbreviation List

HEBREW BIBLE/OLD TESTAMENT

Gen	Genesis
Exod	Exodus
Lev	Leviticus
Num	Numbers
Deut	Deuteronomy
Josh	Joshua
Judg	Judges
1–2 Sam	1–2 Samuel
1–2 Kgs	1–2 Kings
1–2 Chr	1–2 Chronicles
Neh	Nehemiah
Esth	Esther
Ps/Pss	Psalms
Prov	Proverbs
Song	Song of Songs
Isa	Isaiah
Jer	Jeremiah
Ezek	Ezekiel
Dan	Daniel
Hos	Hosea

Obad	Obadiah
Mic	Micah
Nah	Nahum
Hab	Habakkuk
Zeph	Zephaniah
Hag	Haggai
Zech	Zechariah
Mal	Malachi

APOCRYPHA

Bar	Baruch
2 Esd	2 Esdra
Jdt	Judith
1–2, 4 Macc	1–2 Maccabees
3–4	3–4 Maccabees
Sir	Sirach/Ecclesiasticus

TECHNICAL ABBREVIATIONS AND SOURCES

ANET	Pritchard, J., ed. *Ancient Near Eastern Texts Relating to the Old Testament.* Princeton: Princeton University Press, 1969
ARM	Archives royales de Mari
ARMT	Archives royales de Mari, transcrite et traduite
B.C.E.	"Before the Common Era"—used in this book in place of B.C., but the dates are the same
C.E.	"Common Era"—used in this book in place of A.D., but the dates are the same
CH	Code of Hammurabi
Dossin	Dossin, G. "Sur le prophétisme à Mari." Pages 77–86 in *La divination en Mésopotamie ancienne et*

dans les region voisines. Paris: Presses universitaires
de France, 1966

Heb.   Hebrew

OT/HB   Old Testament/Hebrew Bible

OTP   Matthews, V., and D. Benjamin. *Old Testament Parallels: Laws and Stories from the Ancient Near East.* 2d
ed. New York: Paulist, 1997

INTRODUCTION

Examining any text in the Hebrew Bible from a socio-historical perspective requires an understanding that this material has a particular place in history. Writers reflect their own period even when they are editing a narrative originating from an earlier time. Similarly, when prophets speak, they do so within the social and historical context of their own time. They are primarily concerned with current events, not future happenings. Therefore, as we explore the social world of the Hebrew prophets, we must first recognize that these persons, both male and female, spoke within their own time, to an audience with a frame of reference very different from ours.

Although the world of the prophets and their audiences often revolved around urban centers like Jerusalem, Bethel and Samaria, it was agriculturally based. During the period from 1000 to 587 B.C.E., most of the population still lived in small farming communities of 100–250 people. The large number of pastoral and agricultural images employed by the prophets is the best indication of just how intrinsically rural life was in ancient Israel. It would have been counterproductive to speak of herds, vineyards, and summer fruit to people who had no experience of them.

This life was not an easy one: the Mediterranean climate with which these people had to contend brought rain only during the winter months (October through March), and the land they occupied was hilly, badly eroded, and rocky. Thus their lives were hard, often short, and too often dominated by forces beyond their control. In addition, political and economic forces from outside their immediate area added to the pressures of daily existence.

Because we do not share these everyday aspects of ancient existence, one of the greatest challenges for modern readers has been to become acquainted with the social and historical forces that played such an important role in the lives of the prophets and their audiences. With this in mind, I have designed this study to introduce students not only to the Hebrew prophets but also to their social world. In order to accomplish these goals, I will

> introduce each prophet as he or she appears chronologically in the biblical narrative,
>
> sketch out his or her historical context,
>
> explain aspects of historical geography when relevant,
>
> examine the economic and social forces that dominate that particular moment in time,
>
> and explain as many of the images and metaphors utilized by the prophets as possible.

Without a sense of what it meant to be a member of Tekoa's community of hill country farmers and herders or to be an exiled Levite from Anathoth functioning as a prophet in Jerusalem, the reader only skims the surface of the text.

1

HISTORICAL GEOGRAPHY

When the prophets mention a geographic site or feature, they are generally describing a place that they and their audience know intimately. They have walked over each field, climbed the nearby hills, seen the foliage, smelled the various aromas associated with herding sheep or with cultivating an olive orchard or vineyard. Because their frame of reference is that of a geographic "insider," they do not have to go into great detail to conjure up a picture in the minds of their listeners. But this means that modern readers are often lost in the strange-sounding place names and in descriptions of places that are either unknown or so foreign that they cannot even be imagined. In order to acquaint modern readers with this unfamiliar world, I provide here a basic description of the major geographic regions of the ancient Near East and their significance for the Israelites. If additional comment on geography or climate is necessary in describing the words of a particular prophet, I will append it to the relevant chapters below.

The ancient Near East is divided into three primary areas: Mesopotamia, Egypt, and Syria-Palestine. Adjacent to these regions are the Anatolian Peninsula (modern Turkey), Persia (modern Iran), and the island of Cyprus. Each of these subsidiary areas figures in the history and the development of Near Eastern cultures during the biblical period. For instance, the Hittite Empire in Anatolia and portions of Syria and northern Mesopotamia provided a firm cultural link to the Indo-European nations of Europe and also influenced the political development of Syria-Palestine just prior to the emergence of the Israelites in Canaan. Cyprus and the Syrian seaport city of Ugarit functioned as early economic links with the burgeoning Mediterranean civilizations based on Crete and in southern Greece during the second millennium B.C.E. Cyprus was also a prime source of copper, a metal essential to the technology of the Near East for much of its early history. Finally, Persia, in the sixth century B.C.E., developed into the greatest of the Near Eastern empires just as the Israelites were emerging from their Meso-potamian exile. Persian religion (Zoroastrianism) and Persian administrative innovations would contribute to the development of Judaism both in the Diaspora communities and in Palestine.

Travel between and within the various segments of the ancient Near East and the eastern Mediterranean required political cooperation and technological advancements. Early shipping hugged the coasts, but by 2000 B.C.E. ships were making regular stops at the Mediterranean islands as well as up and down the coasts of the Red Sea, the Persian Gulf, and the Indian Ocean. Evi-dence for such far-flung travel can be seen in the list of luxury items and manufactured goods found in the speeches of the prophets.

On land, trade routes generally followed the coasts, where seaports could take raw materials and grain to other markets. In Syria-Palestine, two highways linked Mesopotamia to the Palestin-ian coast and on to Egypt: the **Via Maris** and its extension, the Way of the Philistines, and the King's Highway, which extended from Palmyra to Damascus and south through Transjordan to the Gulf of Aqabah. Caravan routes also followed the Arabian coastline and made it possible for traders to carry frankincense, myrrh, and other exotic goods to Africa and India.

MESOPOTAMIA

The Tigris-Euphrates river valley is the dominant feature in the area known as Mesopotamia. In modern parlance, this region comprises the nation of Iraq as well as parts of Iran and Syria. The river system flows over an increasingly flat expanse of land as it travels from north to south. There is little rainfall in much of this land, but the melting snows in the mountains of eastern Turkey feed the rivers. Life therefore was often precarious, dependent on what little rain did occur and the volume of water available from the rivers and wells. Disaster could strike very quickly in such a fragile environment, where life-giving winds and rain could be replaced by the drying effects of the desert wind, the sirocco.

> Enlil prepares the storm. Let the people mourn. The winds bringing rain to the land, he withholds. Let the people mourn. The good winds he stores in Sumer. Let the people mourn. He gives the burning winds their orders. Let the people mourn. ("Laments for Ur," *OTP*, p. 235)

Cities and towns had to be established on the rivers, and only the introduction of massive irrigation projects made population growth possible. These cooperative efforts eventually served as a major factor in the political development of the region. **City-states** and monarchies appeared very early in Mesopotamian history, while the formation of empires encompassing all or most of Mesopotamia did not occur until the eighteenth century B.C.E.

No major geographic features provide natural barriers or defenses for Mesopotamia. As a result, invasions of new peoples and the rise and fall of civilizations mark the history of the entire area from as early as 4000 B.C.E. The land also did not have an abundance of natural resources. What forests may have existed in great antiquity did not survive into historical times. Mineral resources were found to the north and east of the Tigris-Euphrates Valley, but less so within it. To make up for their lack of natural resources, city-states of Mesopotamia established a brisk river trade to transport goods and raw materials downriver very early in their history. The Mesopotamians also sent caravans into the Arabian Peninsula and east into Persia and the Indus Valley of northwestern India. Such widespread trade links brought a further degree of cultural mixing and created a more **cosmopolitan** culture.

The first civilizations to appear were in the extreme southern area and became known as Sumer (ca. 4000 B.C.E.). These people took advantage of the wetlands and trade links associated with the

Tigris and Euphrates Rivers as they flowed into the Persian Gulf. The city-states of Ur, Kish, Lagash, Nippur, and Uruk dominated this region and were responsible for the invention of the cuneiform writing system, the use of ziggurat towers as part of their temple complexes, and the development of strong monarchies.

Invaders from the steppes of Central Asia brought the first Semitic culture into the area around 2500 B.C.E. This also led to a spread of the population north into the region known as Babylonia. The city of Babylon, located at the point where the Tigris and Euphrates almost meet as they travel south from the Caucasus Mountains, became the center of this new culture and eventually formed the seat of an empire led by Hammurabi (1796–1750 B.C.E.).

The Babylonian Empire did not survive for long, however. Weak leadership, a corrupt or complacent military, or a natural disaster could damage an administration and leave it open to the next wave of invaders. Thus, from 1500 to 1000 B.C.E., no nation was able to dominate the whole area. This ended with the rise of the Assyrians, who occupied the northern reaches of the Tigris. They took advantage of the petty kingdoms that were too busy fighting among themselves to resist an organized and ruthless opponent. Gradually, by 800 B.C.E., the Assyrian **hegemony** came to dominate all of Mesopotamia and then west to the Mediterranean Sea and, at its height in 663, to Egypt. An empire of this size, stretching across more than a thousand miles and many different geographic regions, could only be held together by a policy of systematic terror and immediate retaliation for rebellion.

> The hunter cut open the wombs of the pregnant. He blinded infants. He slit the throats of warriors. . . . Whoever offended Ashur was destroyed. Sing of the power of Assyria, Ashur the strong, who goes forth to battle. ("Annals of Tiglath-pileser I," *OTP*, p. 156)

When the Assyrians failed to maintain this policy, their empire was doomed, and once again they were supplanted for a short period by the Babylonians.

It is possible, however, that the model of empire established and maintained for two hundred years by the Assyrians was the impetus for another imperial power—this time the Persians from east of the Tigris. They recognized the problems created by Assyrian policies and chose to better address their style of empire to the realities of size and space. They invented a "pony express" system that allowed communication to flow over an area of two thousand miles in five days. The Persians also recognized that terror is only effective when constantly in use. As a result, they chose a more benevolent form of administration, allowing freedom of religion and appointing local leaders as Persian representatives whenever possible. Only the rapacious ambitions of Alexander of Macedon could have ended the Persian Empire before its time.

EGYPT

While the Egyptians were able to create an advanced civilization at least as early as that in ancient Sumer, it was very different in character. The differences arise from the more isolated nature of Egypt in relation to the rest of the Near East. On the east, the Red Sea and the wastelands of the Sinai Peninsula provide a very effective barrier to invaders. Once the pharaohs established a line of fortresses to bar the narrow strip of land that connects Egypt and the Sinai, they were able to control almost completely the entrance of armies, migrant peoples, and caravaneers. The Libyan and Sahara deserts protected the western border. Although more open to invasion from Nubia in the south, Egypt was protected, at least by water, by the cataracts of the Nile River.

Nearly all of Egypt's culture and history has developed in, and been sustained by, the Nile river valley. The Nile flows north amid arid wastes and rocky desert outcrops where farmers had to rely entirely on the river for irrigating their fields. As it enters the Mediterranean, the Nile spreads over the land into a fan-shaped delta and is dominated by papyrus marshes. It is customary to refer to the two regions of Egypt as Upper and Lower Egypt. But because the Nile flows from south to north, Upper Egypt is the southern area, from Thebes to Memphis, and Lower Egypt comprises the northern region, including the delta and eastern desert along the Mediterranean coast.

The natural flow of the Nile is interrupted south of Thebes by a series of cataracts that make river traffic nearly impossible. As a result, caravans that brought goods from Arabia, Nubia, and other African kingdoms were forced to follow alongside the Nile rather than travel upon it. This gave the Egyptians a better opportunity to control the influx of people and products and, of course, to tax them. Although smuggling almost certainly occurred, it would have been much more difficult than along the more open borders of Mesopotamia.

Unlike the Tigris-Euphrates river system, which could flood without warning or shift its channel, the Nile was a consistent waterway. Its annual flood cycle was measured early in Egyptian history, and as a result, the people and their rulers were able to plan their agricultural and economic activities with greater certainty than was possible in Mesopotamia. The constancy of life from year to year contributed to a culture that built for the ages and assumed a continuity of existence beyond this life into the next. Just as the Nilotic floods brought new layers of rich topsoil to fertilize and reinvigorate the fields each year, the *ma'at,* or peace, of Egypt was believed to come from the goodwill of the gods and their god-king, the pharaoh.

The Egyptian climate is hot and arid. Daytime temperatures range into the upper 90s F nearly year-round, and this is magnified by the cloudless, sunny skies. It is no wonder, therefore, that the sun god Amon is one of the most powerful of the Egyptian deities. The extreme temperatures do moderate somewhat in the evenings, with cooling breezes coming off the Nile and from the desert. In fact, in the desert it can be quite cold at night. Throughout the region, architectural and clothing styles are based on accommodation to the hot climate.

The extremely small annual rainfall meant that the people relied on the Nile and on wells for their water. As a result, river travel and familiarity with the dangers of the Nile are very common in their literature:

> My lover is a marsh. My lover is lush with growth. . . . Her
> mouth is a lotus bud. Her breasts are mandrake blossoms. . . .

Her head is a trap from branches . . . and I am the goose.
("Egyptian Love Songs," *OTP*, p. 298)

Once, a man plowed his field, loaded the harvest on a barge,
and towed it to market. At sunset, a terrible storm came up.
The man, safe in town, survived, but his wife and children at
home perished, lost when their houseboat capsized in the
Lake of the Crocodiles. ("A Sufferer and a Soul," *OTP*, p. 211)

Metaphors involving the marshes, where birds roost and crocodiles and the hippopotamus are hunted, appear in **genres** as
diverse as love poetry and the teachings of sages.

SYRIA-PALESTINE

Even though Syria-Palestine is the smallest of the Near Eastern regions, it has a much wider variety of topographic features, cli-
mates, and population zones than either Egypt or Mesopotamia.

Syria The northern range of this area included Syria
and the other Aramean states as well as Phoenicia (modern Lebanon). From 1500 to 1200 B.C.E., the Hittite
Empire dominated this northern area, stretching its hegemony
beyond the boundaries of Anatolia (modern Turkey). A significant
economic power during this period was the port city of Ugarit,
which controlled the carrying trade in the eastern Mediterranean.
Ugarit is also responsible for the creation of an alphabetic cuneiform writing system that would dramatically increase literacy
throughout the Near East. Its epic literature has many parallels in
the Psalms and in the prophetic books:

Ba'al proclaimed, "I alone rule the divine assembly. Who but I
can feed the holy ones? Who but I can feed the peoples of the
earth?" ("Ba'al and Anat," *OTP*, p. 251)

May Ba'al the Cloud Rider, and El, the creator of the heavens
and the earth, and every member of the divine assembly erase

the name of that state, and its ruler or strong man. ("Karatepe
Annals of Azitiwada," *OTP*, p. 165)

In fact, the images of **Yahweh** as the master of the storm, the
"Cloud Rider," and the **transcendent** creator God were probably
borrowed from Ugaritic or Canaanite literature and their depictions of the gods El and Baal.

After 1200 B.C.E., a major political and cultural break occurred
in the Near East when a mixed invasion force collectively known as
the Sea Peoples challenged the major cultures. When the dust settled,
Ugarit had been destroyed. Eventually, the Phoenician seaports of
Tyre and Sidon would succeed Ugarit as masters of Mediterranean
shipping. The Hittite Empire was also conquered, leaving the area
in a state of political division that would allow for the Greek colo-
nization of Ionia, the western coast of Anatolia and the offshore
islands.

Egypt was also severely weakened. The abandonment of its
holdings in Canaan created a political vacuum in Canaan that
would eventually be filled by a variety of peoples. These new peoples
included one group of the Sea Peoples, the Philistines. Others may
have been new tribal groups, such as Israel, that infiltrated the virtually empty central hill country and established a tenuous village
culture there. The royal inscription of the pharaoh Merneptah provides at least some basis for this claim of Israel's presence in
Canaan just prior to 1200 B.C.E.:

> I have decimated the people of Israel and put their children to
> death. ("Annals of Merneptah," *OTP*, p. 91)

Other beneficiaries of the new political situation after 1200
B.C.E. were the Phoenicians and the Syrian kingdom around the city
of Damascus. These peoples occupied the area immediately north
and east of Canaan. Phoenicia was blessed with heavily forested
mountain hillsides just inland from a narrow coastal plain that
was only eight to ten miles wide. The cedars had an almost mysti-
cal draw for the nearly treeless countries of Egypt and Mesopotamia and brought great wealth as well as conquering armies to the
Phoenicians and their predecessors.

> The god Nergal did open up the path for the mighty Naram-Sin,
> and gave him Arman and Ibla, and he presented him (also) with

the Amanus, the Cedar Mountain and (with) the Upper Sea. ("Naram-Sin in the Cedar Mountain," *ANET*, p. 268)

I, Wen-Amon, priest at the gate of the temple of Amon, was dispatched to buy timber for the sacred boat of Amon-Ra, ruler of the divine assembly. ("Stories of Wen-Amon," *OTP*, p. 324)

In addition to its wealth of natural resources, Phoenicia possessed several major deep-water port cities, including Byblos, Tyre, and Sidon. Heavily laden ships were able to lie at anchor close to the wharves of these cities as they off-loaded and took on cargo. The wealth that flowed through these ports made them impressive prizes for the growing superpowers in Egypt and Mesopotamia in the period after 900 B.C.E., but for several centuries they were able to operate freely and even to establish merchant colonies in North Africa, Sardinia, and Spain.

Syria (or Aram) was never politically united prior to the Roman period, but the dynasty based at Damascus had influence over much of the region that stretched from the Mediterranean coast on the west to the Taurus Mountains to the north and the Syrian desert on the east. This area encompasses three separate climatic zones: the Mediterranean coastline in the western area; a desert area with less than ten inches of annual rainfall to the south and east; and steppe land between the coast and the desert with sufficient rainfall and other sources of water to support agriculture and small oak forests.

During the eleventh to ninth centuries, Syria was a significant opponent of Israel, as both kingdoms sought to control the lands, north and east of Galilee, that contained the trade routes into and out of Mesopotamia and south through Transjordan. With the advent of camel caravans after 1200 B.C.E. and frequent travel from Mari on the Euphrates west to Tadmor/Palmyra (about 145 miles) and then along a depression between low hills to Damascus (another 130 miles), control of these trade routes became even more desirable. Accordingly, Solomon laid claim to Tadmor and Palmyra (2 Chr 8:4), while the Syrian kings and their aggressive policies were a major concern of the Israelite kings (see 1 Kgs 11:23–25; 15:16–22) and the prophets Elijah and Elisha. The Israelite kings were not always successful in resisting Syrian aggression; in fact, during the latter part of the ninth century, the Syrian king

Hazael was able to successfully invade Israel and Philistia and extend his hegemony over both for a time.

> With Hadad riding before me, I marched out of my land and destroyed seventy rulers with their corps of chariots and horsemen. I put Jehoram, son of Ahab and ruler of Israel, and Ahaziahu, son of Jehoram and ruler of the house of David to death. I destroyed their cities and left their lands barren. ("Tel Dan Annals of Hazael," *OTP*, p. 161)

During the eighth century B.C.E., the Syrians also would figure in the prophetic speech of Isaiah and Amos.

Much of Syria is mountainous. Except in its lower elevations and desert regions, it is subject to extremes of hot and cold temperatures. Like Israel, it was predominately a village culture with agriculture its prime concern. Not surprisingly, therefore, the storm gods Baal and Hadad were of most importance. The major urban center was Damascus, located on the Barada River, on the southwest corner of Syrian territory and virtually on Israel's doorstep.

Palestine

Located on a land bridge between Egypt and Mesopotamia, Palestine is a cultural crossroads as well as a melting pot for many different peoples. It covers only about ten thousand square miles, approximately the size of Vermont or New Hampshire. From north to south, there are only one hundred and forty-five miles between Dan, just north of the Sea of Galilee at the foot of the Hermon mountain range, and Beer-Sheba, on the desert fringe of the eastern Sinai. Traveling west from the coastal plain to Jerusalem is only about thirty miles. From there to the Jordan River is only another twenty miles. Even within this small territory, there are four major geographic zones, each with its own ecological character.

Coastal Plain

The coastal plain consists of a narrow stretch of flat lowlands and sand dune beaches. Because there are no deep-water harbors along this coast, ancient Palestine's commercial efforts were severely limited. Just inland are fertile areas that catch much of the rain and sea breeze from the Mediterranean. In ancient times, there were also some meager forestlands and marshy areas in this area.

The Shephelah lies between the coast and the hill country that bisects the middle of the country. It contains three fertile plains that provide the bulk of Palestine's arable farmland. The first of these is the Plain of Acre, which stretches to the north from Mount Carmel about twenty-five miles and extends inland from five to eight miles. Since this area was controlled by the Phoenicians during the time of the biblical monarchy, it does not figure prominently in the accounts of the court historians or the prophets.

The second of these plains is the Plain of Sharon, which extends to the south of Mount Carmel for nearly fifty miles and about ten miles inland. In antiquity, much of this territory was marshland with few villages except along the coast. As a result, it likewise does not appear to any great extent in the biblical accounts. Just to the south of the Sharon, however, is Philistia, an area settled after 1200 B.C.E. by the Sea Peoples known as Philistines. They either conquered or founded many towns and villages and ruled the area from five major cities. Three of these cities, Ashkelon, Gaza, and Ashdod, were near the coast.

Because much of the coastal plain is quite flat, it naturally became an international trade route used by Egyptians and Mesopotamian merchants as well as their armies. The highway is sometimes referred to as the Via Maris, or "Way of the Sea," but this name probably applies to different links of the road rather than to its entire length. It may be that the Via Maris refers to the portion of the road that extended from the coast east through the Valley of Jezreel, south of the Carmel range of mountains, and then on north through Galilee to Damascus. This detour from the northern route was made necessary by the fact that the Carmel range extends to within 150 yards of the Mediterranean. Such a narrow band would have been a perfect place for ambushes. Consequently, Megiddo, the site where the Jezreel Valley opens to the east, became the gatekeeper to the trade route.

> Behold, all foreign countries have been put in this town by the command of Re on this day, inasmuch as every prince of every northern country is shut up within it, for the capturing of

> Megiddo is the capturing of a thousand towns! ("The Asiatic Campaigns of Thut-mose III," *ANET*, p. 237)

The summer temperatures along the coastal plain are quite hot, averaging about 100° during the day. A sea breeze in the evenings makes this more tolerable, but the architecture and business practices had to cope with a portion of the day when it was simply too hot to move. During the winter months (the period when most rainfall occurs) the temperatures dip into the 40s and 50s, but there is no danger of frost to harm plants. As a result, two grain harvests can be expected each year, and all types of fruit trees (among them olive, date, fig, and pomegranate) grow well here.

> October to sow the barley, December and January to sow the wheat....March and April to harvest the barley, April to harvest the wheat and to feast. ("Gezer Almanac," *OTP*, p. 146)

Central Hill Country   The spine of hills that runs from north to south down the middle of Palestine is called the central hill country. It rises from the rolling hills of the Shephelah Plateau to elevations of as much as thirty-three hundred feet above sea level between Hebron and Jerusalem. This narrow region would ultimately form the heart of both Israel and Judah during the monarchy. It only began to be settled with any degree of density starting in the Iron Age (around 1100 B.C.E.). The appearance of numerous village sites after that point suggests an influx of population, probably related to the settlement of the Philistines along the coast and in the Shephelah. The hills themselves were denuded of trees in antiquity, and many of the hillsides were badly eroded. This may explain why much of the area was not settled by the Canaanites. In any case, it would have provided a safe, if not easy, life for refugees as well as new immigrants.

As is the case with all of Palestine's regions, the central hill country must also be subdivided as one moves from north to south. The climate becomes increasingly hot and dry in the southern reaches. In the north, in the Galilee region and the Valley of Jezreel, there is adequate rainfall to support agriculture, and there is sufficient arable land in the valleys and basins to provide for the needs of both village communities and larger urban centers such as Megiddo and Beth-shean.

The middle portion of the hill country, which stretches from Dothan to Bethel, contains a number of large cities, including Israel's capital, Samaria, and the **cultic** site of Shechem. Although not as lush as Galilee, this central area contained a large population during the monarchic period and was the location of many important events and battles. Agriculture here had to rely more heavily on terraced hillsides, since there was less flat land. Fig and olive trees were abundant, and there was adequate pasturage for herds of sheep and goats.

The southernmost section of the hill country included the territory of Judah, with Jerusalem, Hebron, and the Judean wilderness. Because of the higher elevations, this region experiences greater temperature extremes than the rest of the country. In the hot and dry summers, the temperature is often in the 90s, while in the wet months of winter, the people shiver at night with blustery winds and temperatures in the 30s and 40s. Significant snowfall in Jerusalem is not unusual, and frost is a common morning experience.

Jordan River Valley   The Jordan river valley lies farther to the east. It was created by a gigantic rift or a geological fault in the earth that starts in Syria and extends south all the way to the Red Sea and Africa. Much of this huge fold in the earth is below sea level, although there are a few areas, such as the Huleh Basin just ten miles north of the Sea of Galilee, that have a slightly higher elevation (230 feet above sea level). For instance, despite being surrounded by steep hills, the Sea of Galilee is 700 feet below sea level. From that point, elevations continue to decrease along the course of the Jordan River.

The Jordan River originates north of the Sea of Galilee and is fed by springs at several sources, among them Tel Dan and Banias/Caesarea Philippi, and by the melting snows of the Hermon Range. It flows into the Sea of Galilee and then meanders south over a distance of about seventy miles. Its actual course, however, is so circuitous that the banks of the waterway here stretch nearly two hundred miles. Several well-known fords along the Jordan are mentioned as strategic sites in the biblical narrative (see Judg 3:28; 12:5–6).

The Dead Sea is the repository of the Jordan's flow. It is the lowest spot on the face of the earth, about twenty-six hundred feet below sea level at its northernmost end. The water is trapped here without an outlet and quickly evaporates in the extremely high temperatures of the area. The result is an extremely high salt content that transforms the lake into a health spa of great value, but it also deprives the lake of any life forms. The most important settlement near the northern end of the Dead Sea is the oasis community of Jericho. Since it receives only about two inches of rainfall per year, its existence as a continually occupied site for over ten thousand years is due to the continuous springs. Other important sites around the Dead Sea that play a role in biblical history, including Qumran and Ein-gedi, are also supported by springs.

Unlike the Tigris-Euphrates system and the Nile River, the Jordan River cuts its banks so deeply that it is difficult to create extensive irrigation projects. It is prohibitively expensive in time and funds to raise the water up over the riverbank, and as a result, there is less irrigation farming and there are fewer settlements along the southern range of the Jordan River. The high temperatures, which average over 100° for much of the year, and the nearly complete lack of rainfall also cut down on population growth during the biblical period. To be sure, there would be a number of events in this area, but they tended to center on the idea of "wilderness" rather than the normal pursuits of life.

Transjordanian   The last of the Syro-Palestinian regions to be
Plateau   considered is the Transjordanian Plateau, which
                       runs for about 250 miles from Mount Hermon in the north to the Gulf of Aqabah in the south. The region consists of a narrow plateau and set of hills running east from 30 to 80 miles to the eastern desert.

Transjordan includes two Israelite territories. Farthest north are the Golan Heights, which include the oak forests (Ezek 27:6) and lush mountain pasturelands of Bashan just to the east of the

Galilee region (see Ezek 39:18) and extending south to the Yarmuk River. The other is the region just to the east of the Jordan known as Gilead, where some of the tribes are said to have settled after the conquest in Joshua's time (Josh 17:6). It is a mountainous region with a number of V-shaped valleys lying between the Yarmuk and the northern end of the Dead Sea. It is bisected from east to west by the very steep Jabbok river valley. Like Bashan, the Gilead region has sufficient rainfall to support wheat farming as well as the cultivation of olive trees and grape orchards.

Farther south and east, between the Jabbok and the Arnon Rivers, is the kingdom of Ammon. Its capital at Rabbah anchored a state that stretched along a narrow, fertile band of land between Gilead and the eastern desert. While the kingdom was supposed to be bounded by the eastern arm of the Jabbok River, **archaeological** evidence has shown Ammonite sites west of this area. Since it lay on the plateau above the hills associated with the Jordan Valley, Ammon and especially Rabbah became prosperous as a link on the King's Highway.

The area between the very deep valley of the Arnon River and the River Zered formed the boundaries of Moab. It is mountainous country, with elevations to thirty-six hundred feet above sea level. Although it is watered by springs, the average annual rainfall decreases in its southern reaches. As a result, much of this southern region is given over to sheep and goat herding, while agriculture is possible closer to the Arnon. A tableland area, the Mishor, adjoins Moab to the west. It stretches from the Heshbon in the north for about twenty-five miles south to Aroer and Dibon, just north of the Arnon Valley. Among the sites located here were Mount Nebo and Shittim. A territory disputed between Moab and Israel, it was controlled by Moab during most of the period of the divided monarchy (Isa 15:4–9; Jer 48:2–5; Ezek 25:8–11).

> Chemosh said to me, "Go, take Nebo from Israel." . . . I built Aroer and a highway through the Arnon Valley. I also rebuilt the cities of Beth-bamoth and Bezer for fifty households from Dibon. ("Annals of Mesha," *OTP*, pp. 158–59)

Edom, the southernmost Transjordanian kingdom, was located in a region between the Zered River and the Gulf of Aqabah. It is mountainous country, with peaks as much as fifty-seven hundred feet above sea level; its cities were built along the narrow ridges of these hills. The living area for Edom was further narrowed by the Arabah, an extension of the Jordan Rift, to the west and by the eastern desert on the east. This left only about twelve or thirteen miles of inhabitable area east to west for the Edomites. The western crest of these mountain ridges receives enough rainfall to support agriculture, but at lower elevations it is quite dry, supporting only scrub forests and marked by the exposure, due to erosion, of limestone cliffs and Nubian sandstone. The red color of this landscape gave Edom its name, since "Edom" means "red" in Hebrew.

Travel through this rugged land was extremely difficult. Only the pass at Punon (Num 33:42), twenty-five miles south of the Zered, affords passage from the Arabah east for nine miles. The northern area of Edom, sometimes referred to as Teman, was dominated by fortresses such as Bozrah (Amos 1:12). These sites adjoined and guarded the southern portion of the King's Highway as it extended on to the Gulf of Aqabah.

This overview has provided only a cursory description of the major geographical and geopolitical regions of the ancient Near East; nevertheless it should serve as a reminder of the complexity of the world of the Hebrew prophets. The social world of which they were a part, is governed like our own, in large part by their interaction with the environment's barriers, potentials, and limitations. Because the prophets constantly refer to geographical regions, cities, and landmarks, a basic knowledge of these features is essential for anyone who studies their words and writings.

2

DEFINING AND DESCRIBING
THE PROPHET

WHAT WAS A PROPHET?

There is a long history of prophetic activity in the ancient Near East. Much of this activity is associated with practices of **divination** and the interpretation of omens. Because Mesopotamian religion assumes that the gods represent the forces of nature and are therefore both powerful and capricious, the determination of the future by the reading of omens is critical. No army went to war, no temple or other public building was constructed, and no diplomatic marriage was arranged without first consulting the omens. As a result, a whole industry developed of persons who could interpret the visible symbols of the gods' intentions.

The task of the diviner is to determine the will of a god or gods through various ritualized actions, such as the examination of sheep entrails, consultation with the dead (1 Sam 28:8), or the study of the astrological configurations. Over the generations, the nature of these omens and their possible interpretations were recorded in what are now called omen texts. These texts, along with clay models of sheep livers, were then studied by priests-in-training, who would consult the ancient documents first before making any pronouncement.

Ezekiel 21:21 contains a striking example of a Mesopotamian king's use of various forms of divination. Here the Babylonian king Nebuchadnezzar employs three separate techniques—shaking a group of arrows and then choosing one (belomancy); consulting the teraphim, or divine images that he has brought with the army; and, finally, examining a sheep liver (hepatoscopy).

Israelite law forbade all of these practices because they were associated with false gods and false religions (see Deut 18:10–13). There was also an implicit recognition that the practice of divination could be corrupted by a diviner's desire to please his clients (see 1 Kgs 22:1–8). Thus prophets like Jeremiah condemned such practices (see Jer 27:9–10).

Biblical writers also remembered, however, diviners such as Balaam (Num 22–24), who were not just religious practitioners following a prescribed set of texts to interpret the will of the gods but also seemed deeply moved by dreams and **oracles** that came spontaneously from God.

> This is the story of Balaam, son of Beor and a seer. The divine assembly appeared to Balaam, son of Beor, at night. He dreamed he heard El pronounce a death sentence on his city. . . . When Balaam got up the next morning, he began to fast and to lament bitterly. The people of the city asked: "Balaam, son of Beor, why do you fast? Why do you mourn?" So Balaam agreed to tell them about his dream. ("Stories of Balaam," *OTP*, pp. 124–25)

These persons, both male and female, were recognized as prophets, or spokespersons for a god or gods. Some are defined as ecstatic, while others are less spectacular divine spokespersons. But they all deliver messages from one or more gods. Among the ancient texts that best describe these ancient prophets are the letters from the eighteenth-century B.C.E. government archive at Mari, a city on the northern Euphrates River where it borders Syria and Iraq today. At least three classes of male and female prophets advised king Zimri-Lim. *Apilum* prophets spoke for the divine assembly and thus made formal statements and held high status. They were not required, however, to serve within the temple or **cultic** community. *Assinu* prophets were temple personnel, and so their messages most often dealt with cultic matters, such as the rebuilding of a temple or the making of an annual or memorial sacrifice. *Muhhu* prophets were ecstatics who spoke while in a trance brought on by drugs, physical deprivation, or music. It is unclear whether they were associated with the temple. It is quite likely, however, that their frenzied statements were interpreted and transmitted to the king by the priests or government officials.

Since prophetic activity very often included either a trance state or an ecstatic experience, it is not surprising that in Mari the word for "prophet" means "epileptic" and the hieroglyphic sign for "prophet" in the Egyptian "Memoirs of Wen-Amon" is a human figure in convulsions. Biblical prophets induce ecstasy with music (2 Kgs 3:15), dancing (1 Kgs 18:26), or a combination of the two (1 Sam 10:5, 10). The personal names of the nonbiblical prophets never appear in the letters, which could indicate that they were considered members of a sacred social class whose names could not be spoken.

WHO WERE THE HEBREW PROPHETS?

Although the Hebrew prophets resemble the diviners of the ancient Near East in some respects, the biblical writers remembered them as more than religious practitioners. While some of them were members of the priestly community, the prophets stood outside that institution. They occasionally interpreted omens, but they were not diviners, and their message was never totally dependent on the examination of physical clues to God's behavior or intention. Rather, their role was to challenge the establishment and the social order, to remind the leadership and the people of their obligation to the **covenant** with **Yahweh,** and to warn the people of punishment that would surely ensue if they violated this covenant.

The Prophetic Role In the world of ancient Israel, the prophet may *not* be identified as simply a fortune-teller, a social activist, a doomsayer, a messenger, a moralist, or even a predictor of Jesus. Part of the difficulty stems from the fact that the word "prophet" is used in a variety of ways in the Hebrew Bible. Here are a few examples of the range of uses: Abraham (Gen 20:7), Moses (Deut 18:18), Aaron (Exod 4:14–16), and Miriam (Exod 15:20) are called prophets in the **Pentateuch** even though they are more properly considered ancestors. And while Deborah (Judg 4:4) and Samuel are also called prophets, it is better to think of them as heroes. In the late historical work known as Chronicles, the Levites, who were temple functionaries, are called prophets (1 Chr 25). Finally, the **canon** includes the books of Haggai, Zechariah, and Malachi with the prophets even though they were visionaries.

Figuring out what a prophet *is*, however, is often more difficult than stating what a prophet is not. Consider the following six propositions as we define the prophet's role.

(1) Although some Hebrew prophets experienced ecstasy, it does not appear to have been essential. Ecstasy threw prophets into seizures or convulsions and was therefore a sign, in the ancient world, of being possessed by God. While several prophets did experience such ecstatic states, many did not.

(2) Prophetic speech, in whatever form, was a strategy for crisis management that was closely associated with the time of the monarchies of Israel and Judah (1000–587 B.C.E.). Throughout this period, wars and taxes plunged the two small countries into one crisis after another. Crisis, by definition, often destroys the old rules and throws a culture into chaos. Prophets appeared at these times, and their pronouncements often analyzed the nation's prospects for survival.

(3) Prophets always challenged the monarchs of Israel and Judah, even when they were speaking directly to the people. In this respect, their strategy was like that employed by the Assyrian ambassador who challenged King Hezekiah by negotiating directly with the people of Jerusalem during a siege (2 Kgs 18:13–37).

(4) The confrontations between monarchs and prophets were not simply personality conflicts but were instead part of a sociopolitical process that prevented the monarchs from becoming absolute. It would be wrong to conclude that prophets spoke for Yahweh and the monarchs did not. Both were committed to

fulfilling Yahweh's covenant with Israel. They would agree that the same God who cared for the ancestors and who fed and protected the Hebrews in the wilderness was responsible for the kingdoms of Israel and Judah. They disagreed on which systems best reflected that conviction. These disagreements tended to be played out in the analysis of economic, judicial, and administrative systems.

Economic systems. Monarchs viewed themselves as Yahweh's stewards, responsible for feeding and protecting their countries; they utilized the centralized economy common in most Canaanite **city-states.** By contrast, the prophets saw themselves as sentries (Jer 1:11–13) protecting the ideals of the covenant and the older subsistence economy that had been common in the premonarchic period (1250–1000 B.C.E.). A similar balance of power between a prophet and a king existed in Mari, where Nur-Sin, an official of Zimri-Lim, the king of Mari, reported:

> An apilum prophet of Addu, God of Halab, said to me: "Am I not Addu, God of Halab, who has raised you . . . who helped you regain your father's throne? I never ask too much of you. Respond to the appeals of your people when they experience injustice and give them a just verdict." (A.2925, in Dossin, p. 78)

Royal administration. Monarchs defended the state by collecting taxes, raising armies, and making **treaties.** In response, prophets asserted that such actions usurped Yahweh's authority and exclusive right to feed and protect Israel. The confrontation between David and the prophet Gad is typical (2 Sam 24:1–25). David had taken a military census in order to muster an army to protect Israel. But Gad denounced David's action as treason and reminded him that only Yahweh, and not the king, protected Israel: "[W]ill you flee three months before your foes . . . or shall there be three days' pestilence in your land?" Furthermore, only Yahweh, and not the king, could feed the people: "Shall three years of famine come to you in your land?"

As if to underscore this point, the climax of the narrative is set at a threshing floor where food is processed and taxes collected. This installation symbolizes the power of God to feed the nation (2 Sam 25:16–17). Gad's sentence reminds David that without God's help he is powerless to protect and to feed himself and his people.

Judicial systems. There were two judicial systems in ancient Israel. Each was a separate system, and although they functioned side by side, one did not review or appeal to the other. Although prophets were associated with both systems, monarchs figured prominently in one system, while prophets were more frequently found in the other.

In one judicial system, monarchs administered courts martial. In a court martial, the plaintiff went before the monarch, who alone heard the petition and rendered a verdict that could be enforced by police power. Courts martial were concerned primarily with matters of taxation, political crimes, and military service. The prophet Nathan (2 Sam 12:1–25) and the wise woman of Tekoa (2 Sam 14:1–33) were plaintiffs in this court, and Elijah appealed the sentence that a court martial carried out on Naboth (1 Kgs 21).

In another judicial system, prophets were associated with the gate court and the court of the Divine Assembly. The gate court antedated the monarchy and continued to serve as a rival center of power throughout the period of the monarchy. Prophets associated themselves with the gate court to emphasize their function in balancing the power of the monarchs (Jer 19). Like any other citizen, prophets would often stand at a gate to initiate their course of action (Jer 7:1–2). The venue of the trial at a gate court was regularly transferred to the **Divine Assembly** (1 Kgs 22:1–40; Ps 82:1), which is analogous to the gate court in several different ways. Powerful landowners made up the gate court, while Yahweh, the heavens, the earth, and the prophets made up the Divine Assembly. Both courts convened at boundaries: the gate court convened at the boundary between the cosmos within and the chaos outside, while the Divine Assembly met at the boundary between the divine and human planes. Both had the task of resolving disputes involving land and children. Residents of a single city appeared before the gate court; nations before the Divine Assembly.

In addition, the Divine Assembly convened to renew treaties during elaborate **liturgies** at royal sanctuaries. Prophets used a **genre** called a covenant lawsuit to try monarchs who did not fulfill their treaty obligations. Within this context, the Divine Assembly served as the jury whose decision the prophets announced to Israel and Judah in the form of an **oracle** (Mic 3).

Conduct of warfare. War also brought monarchs and prophets into confrontation. In premonarchic Israel, only Yahweh could declare war. A hero would then be lifted up to help deliver the people with the assistance of the **Divine Warrior.** The monarchy replaced these defensive wars with standing professional armies sent into battle, as a part of royal strategy and diplomacy. Prophets remained part of the protocol of war even after the establishment of the monarchy. No king would consider going into battle without making a sacrifice and determining whether Yahweh would assist his army (1 Kgs 22:1–40). The **oracles against foreign nations** (Amos 1:3–2:16; Ezek 25–28), the Day of Yahweh traditions (Isa 13:6; Joel 1:15), and the **motif** of the enemy from the north (Jer 1:14) all played a part in mustering troops for battle—although not always Israelite troops!

(5) The prophet was not just a messenger for the Divine Assembly. Messengers were an important, but a different, part of the biblical world. In Mesopotamia, *mar šipri* messengers were responsible for communications and negotiations between monarchs. *Suharu* messengers ran letters from one ruler to the other (ARM 12.131), usually announcing the arrival of an important official or a foreign army. *Ša sikkim* messengers served as proxies for their monarchs. They carried letters of introduction outlining the royal prerogatives that they enjoyed, which could include authorization to draft treaties (ARM 2.77). Hosts lavished them with food, clothing, and slaves, sensing that to honor a monarch's messenger was to honor that king himself (ARM 12.747). They also provided them with bodyguards and escorts (ARM 6.14:22–28) to protect them from harm while they were in the country (ARMT 14.58:5–15), and to prevent them from spying as they traveled through it (ARM 2.41:3′–4′). Meticulously kept records note the names, destinations, and backgrounds of all of the messengers who come and go (ARM 6.14). For strategic and political reasons, a host could temporarily delay messengers, but not permanently detain them (ARMT 14.97:5–14).

Only two of the twenty references in the Bible to messengers refer to prophets as messengers (Hag 1:13; Mal 3:1). Messengers and prophets are both representatives, but messengers represent monarchs, whereas prophets represent the Divine Assembly. Both the monarchs and the Divine Assembly commission representatives with the formula "Go to [proper name] and say . . . ," but messengers carry information, whereas prophets deliver a legal verdict (Jonah 1:2). Both are treated with the respect or disdain due those they represent, but messengers play no role in the development of, or the response to, the communications they carry. Prophets take an active part both in the deliberations of the Divine Assembly and in working out Israel's response (Amos 7:1–9). As such, although they carry a message, they also function as envoys or ambassadors of Yahweh and thus benefit from a form of diplomatic immunity (Jer 26:12–15).

(6) Prophets generated a wide range of reactions. In some cases, the word "prophet" is derogatory. For example, Amaziah, a priest at Bethel, calls Amos a prophet (Amos 7:10–17), and the context suggests that this is not a good thing. Similarly, the **Septuagint,** the Greek translation of the Old Testament, calls Hananiah a "prophet" (Jer 35:1). In both of these contexts, the term "prophet" refers to a sort of court prophet, who is a bureaucrat or royal consultant, not an independent, reliable agent of God (1 Kgs 22:5–6). What distinguishes true prophets from false prophets is not their means of support but their interpretation of Israel's prospects for survival, based on the degree to which Israel is in compliance with the covenant.

Conclusions   Prophets were not eccentrics who plagued the biblical world with their visions or erratic behavior. They were important players in the struggle for survival. The ecstasy that overpowered the prophets identified them as channels linking the human community with the divine. Their actions and their words offered the human community a fleeting glimpse of the consequences of the actions of their rulers. The Hebrew prophets were powerful because they were sensitive not only to the precarious balance of power between Yahweh and the monarchs but also to the people's obligation to Yahweh under the covenant. They could feel and communicate the repercussions of a single act of royal power on the nations in the days ahead.

CHARACTERISTICS OF PROPHECY

The characteristics described in this section are not exhaustive, nor will every prophet exhibit every characteristic. Nevertheless, the reader should become familiar with these factors and be able to recognize them when they appear in the biblical text or in extrabiblical materials.

The Prophet's Call   Call stories imitate the installation of an ambassador. The intention of the stories is to confer authority on the prophet, not to provide biographical information. These narratives authorize the prophets' monitoring of Israel's compliance with its **covenant** with **Yahweh**. Thus the **call** is the distinctive event that marks the occasion when a person becomes a prophet. Some stories, such as that of Moses, are quite elaborate. And when the biblical writer includes a detailed description of a call, it is usually intended to enhance the importance of the prophet as well as the prophet's message.

The stories of the calls of Isaiah, Jeremiah, and Ezekiel were told by Israelites who had witnessed the coronation of monarchs and were influenced by this experience. The literary pattern in these stories includes a series of steps:

A divine encounter or **theophany** (Isa 6:1–2);

An introductory word or greeting (Isa 6:3–5);

An objection or demurral (Isa 6:4–5);

A commissioning statement (Isa 6:9–10);

A sign or talisman empowering the person who has been chosen (Isa 6:11–13).

The call transforms the individual. This person, who may have been undistinguished to this point in his or her life, now becomes a dynamic spokesperson for God. The call invests the new prophet with special powers, a message, and a mission.

In addition to describing the prophet's call, the call story also highlights the majesty of God. Mountains shake from their foundations. Clouds or fog obscure human vision, earthquakes rumble, and divine beings, including angels, appear in theophanic manifestation. The immediate reaction of the human to all this power is abject fear. For example, Ezekiel falls to the ground, Moses hides his face, and Isaiah stands in amazement that he has survived this encounter.

The introductory word or greeting that follows the theophany discloses God's name and God's reason for appearing at this time and place. The naming is necessary because the Israelites lived their entire existence within a polytheistic milieu. All the other nations had many gods, and it would have been only natural to wonder which god had appeared. Moses, for example, asks God's name because he knows that the Hebrews will want to know (Exod 3:13).

The reason for appearing establishes the basis for the prophet's mission. Yahweh has identified a problem, and since it is always the role of the "chosen people" to deal with their own problems (especially if they are the cause of the problem), one of their own people will be sent to provide a warning. The warning is necessary since, by definition, Yahweh is a righteous God. Although Yahweh may indeed destroy the wicked, he must give righteous humans a warning that will allow them to rectify the problem and thereby save their own lives. A good example of such a warning is God's disclosure to the righteous Noah of the coming flood that is intended to cleanse the earth of wickedness (Gen 6:9–18). The deliverance of the righteous from judgment becomes the basis for the **remnant** theme described below.

Perhaps because it is only natural or perhaps because a formal literary **motif** has been created to frame these narratives, the human who has been singled out by God now demurs and protests that he is unworthy or incapable of doing the job. For instance, Jeremiah claims that he is too young and does not know how to speak in public (Jer 1:6). God sweeps aside these excuses with assurances of support and the provision of special powers or signs. The latter aspect is more applicable to Moses than to the later prophets.

Among the methods of dealing with the demurral is an empowering event. Isaiah, for instance, claims that he is not worthy to accept God's call or speak God's words because he has "unclean lips" (Isa 6:5). This means that his mortal lips could never be spiritually pure enough to speak holy words. The solution is for an angel to take a hot coal from the sacrificial brazier near the altar and symbolically cauterize Isaiah's lips. This is not a physical burning but a spiritual purification that occurs in a vision, not in reality.

Once God has dispensed with the human's excuses, God discloses the prophet's mission. This charge identifies the prophet with the call to mission and the message to be delivered.

The Prophet's Compulsion

There is a special compulsion associated with the call to be a prophet. It can be denied for a time, but ultimately it must be answered. For example, Jonah attempts to flee from his commission, but eventually he must fulfill God's command to preach judgment to the city of Nineveh (Jonah 1:13–17). The compulsion also includes the need to speak. Many of the call stories include a reassurance that God will give the prophet the words that are to be spoken (Exod 4:12; Jer 1:7–9). Although a prophet might be reluctant to speak harsh words or condemn his people, he experiences a compulsion to speak that he cannot resist (Jer 20:9).

Sometimes a prophet's speaking is completely under God's control. Ezekiel, for example, is restrained from speaking any words of comfort or hope during the first portion of his ministry (Ezek 3:25–27). After Jerusalem falls to Nebuchadnezzar's army in 587 B.C.E., Ezekiel can then speak a more reassuring message that promises an eventual end to the exile and a restoration of the covenant between Yahweh and his people.

The Prophet's Message

A prophet's message was always spoken in the name of God. A prophet never introduced his message with the words "Thus says Amos" or "Thus says Isaiah." Rather, the messenger formula is always, "Thus says the LORD [Yahweh]" (see Mic 2:3; Jer 5:14). The message is thus the most important thing about the prophet, not the prophet himself or herself. This may be why prophets rarely mentioned specific names or dates that could draw the people away from the central core of the message. Certainly, there were some prophets, such as Balaam (Num 22:4–6) and Elijah (1 Kgs 18:17), who became famous in their own right, but this was based on their message or their ability to speak for God.

Some prophets do stand out as individuals. Isaiah parades through the streets naked. Jeremiah cries out his frustration from his prison cell and the public stocks. Ezekiel performs acts out of character for a priest. But no matter how odd they act or how flamboyant they may appear, what is at stake is ensuring that the people receive the message of God. Any outrageous acts they perform are designed to attract the people's attention to that message.

The Truthfulness of the Prophet's Message   For a prophet to gain credibility with the people, the message must come true. The Deuteronomic tradition regarding prophets in Deut 13:1–4 cautions against prophets who call on the people to "follow other gods"; and Deut 18:18–22 states that a true prophet speaks in Yahweh's name alone and that the prophet's words come true. This is one reason prophets declare that they speak a message that comes from God. By doing this, they separate themselves from their words and thus cannot be charged with treason, sedition, or doom saying. It is also why some prophets speak ambiguous messages that can be interpreted in more than one way.

The greatest measure of trust and authority, however, comes to the prophet who takes the dangerous path of speaking about the present or the near future. Doing this, the prophet must face the hostility of the people who will eventually experience the punishment expressed in the prophetic message. The prophet may, however, be incarcerated or undergo a trial by ordeal from the time the message is first delivered until it is or is not fulfilled (see 1 Kgs 22:26–28).

Meanwhile, those who hear the prophetic message must decide whether to obey prophetic instructions or to reject them on the chance that the prophet is not a legitimate spokesperson for God. It is even possible that two prophets will speak contradictory messages, creating **cognitive dissonance,** a condition in which the prophetic messages both appear to be true and can only be tested by actual events (see Jer 28).

Prophetic Vocabu-   It is only natural that the prophets would
lary and Genres   speak in the language of the people being
                         addressed and would use images and vocabu-
lary that these people would find familiar (see Ezek 33:5–6). We also need to contend with the fact of historical change during the prophetic period. These prophets operated over a period of about six hundred years, and the social and political situations changed drastically during these centuries. As the times changed, the prophets' audiences also changed, and so did their images and vocabulary.

Nevertheless, one way that a prophet identified himself or herself as a prophet was by using the images or language of a previous prophet. It is not uncommon for one prophet to make statements similar to those of earlier prophets or to have some portion of his or her career (very often the call story) parallel that of past prophets, especially Moses (Deut 18:15). For instance, Isaiah's call story (Isa 6:1–4) contains a visual image of the earthquake and smoke familiar from Moses' Sinai theophany. Similarly, several prophets employ the "**oracle** against the nations" theme as part of their message (Amos, Isaiah, Jeremiah, and Ezekiel).

Of course, prophets did introduce or emphasize particular phrases that became their identifying rhetorical marker. For example, Ezekiel frequently employs the recognition formula, "then they shall know that I am the LORD" (cf. Ezek 7:27; 26:6; 36:11). Although this phrase is used a few times in other prophetic texts (Isa 52:6; Hos 8:2; Joel 3:17), it seems to serve as a literary glue in Ezekiel, tying together his message and reinforcing his theme of God's self-disclosure in the events of Ezekiel's time.

One example of the use of similar phrases or terms by various prophets is the phrase "all flesh." It appears most often in the latter chapters of Isaiah (Isa 40:5, 6; 49:26; 66:16, 23, 24), which date to the period of the end of the exile (ca. 540 B.C.E.). It is also found, however, in the writings of the exilic prophets Jeremiah (Jer 25:31; 32:27; 45:5) and Ezekiel (Ezek 20:48; 21:4, 5), as well as in the writings of the postexilic prophets Zechariah (Zech 2:13) and Daniel (Dan 4:12). What seems clear here is that this favorite phrase has become "stock-in-trade" language for prophets from the period after 600 B.C.E.

Prophetic words often mimic the official language that monarchs use to officiate at a funeral, deliver a proclamation, ratify a **treaty,** promulgate law, conduct worship, or declare war. In every area of life where monarchs spoke, prophets challenged. The use of woe or **lament** oracles associates prophets with funerals (Ezek 24:9–10). The parable and the proverb, with their association with **wisdom** (Ezek 18:2–4), tie the prophets with the royal court (Isa 5). The miracle story, with its emphasis on individual acts of assistance, is associated with village justice (2 Kgs 4:1–7). A call story parallels royal diplomacy and accession to power (Jer 1). The covenant lawsuit (Hos 4:1–4), the oracle, or the juridical verdict ties them to the gate court (1 Kgs 22:10–17), and the oracle against the nations or **execration rituals** signal the prophet's prediction of war (Jer 46:13–26). Each of these types of prophetic statement is associated with the power of Yahweh alone to feed and protect the people.

What distinguishes a prophet from other prophets is most often the historical context of his message. Elijah speaks to Ahab, not to some future monarch of Israel. Isaiah's reference to the Syro-Ephraimitic war in Isa 7 speaks to a specific historical event. Haggai's pronouncement on the need to reconstruct the temple in Jerusalem fits only into the immediate postexilic period and the rule of the governor Zerubbabel.

To be sure, the prophets make references to the activities of previous prophets, but not usually by name (Amos 2:11; Zech 1:3–4). Instead there is an established tradition—the continuity of the prophetic movement and of the message that the prophets bring from Yahweh, stretching back from their own day into the earliest history of the people.

Enacted Prophecies   Prophets were masters of both the silent and the sounded arts. Not only did they speak; they also performed symbolic actions. Symbolic actions are pantomimes. Prophets used three kinds of pantomimes. There are single dramatic gestures; for instance, Jeremiah buries his clothes in the riverbank (Jer 13:1–11). Austere practices or asceticism can be employed, as when Jeremiah refuses to marry and attend funerals or celebrations (Jer 16:1–13). Or a prophet may identify with the silent actions or craft of another, as when Jeremiah, like a teacher, draws the attention of his audience to the potter at his wheel (Jer 18:2–4).

Pantomime is the ancient and universal art of gesture, an expression of social interaction. Anthropologists, sociologists, and dramatists continue to identify a wide variety of pantomimes first celebrated in the cave paintings of the Stone Age and found also in the magic, ritual, and dances of traditional societies. Technically, pantomime is theater without script. Performers in masks may even use words and music to accompany their gestures. But mime is primarily a spectacle, an art whose medium is movement and that appeals to the sense of sight. Pantomime grew from a conviction in traditional cultures that only gesture, acrobatics, and dance can appropriately address human realities.

For the prophets, pantomime was not solely representational art. It was also, like the Ghost Dance of 1890, an act or set of acts that was believed to be able to set events in motion. Prophetic symbolic acts could act as catalysts for social change. The message of change sometimes required overt action to throw off physical or cultural oppression or to restore a lost commitment to the covenant and its obligations.

Male and Female Prophets Both men and women functioned as prophets; no distinction seems to have been drawn between them as to authority or authenticity. Indeed, the prophet Huldah herself acts as an authenticator of a tradition associated with Moses (2 Kgs 22:14–20). This is in tune with the appearance of both male and female prophets elsewhere in the ancient Near East. Since it was understood that prophets had been chosen by a god to serve as their mouthpiece, their individual characteristics, including gender, had no bearing on the message. This is further evidence of the fact that prophets were not chosen for their self-importance, status, or personal abilities.

Modes of Prophetic   Prophetic speech was elicited in a variety of
Utterance   ways and uttered in several different styles. It
                       was sometimes the result of a physical trance
state (Ezek 8:1; 11:1-5) that occasionally was induced by music
and/or dancing (1 Sam 10:5, 10; 2 Kgs 3:15). Most often, however,
prophecy was simply spoken as a report of a vision (1 Kgs
22:19-22) or of the words of God, as spoken to the prophet.

Prophetic words borrowed **genres** from a variety of social
institutions. The woe or lament oracle portrayed the prophet as a
mourner (Ezek 24:9-10). The parable and the proverb cast the
prophet as a teacher (2 Sam 12:1-15). The miracle story and the
call story paralleled the prophet with a monarch (2 Kgs 4:1-7; Jer
1:14-19). The covenant lawsuit and the oracle regarded the
prophet as a member of the **Divine Assembly** (1 Kgs 22:10-7; Hos
4:1-4). Oracles against the nations portrayed the prophet as a
judge pronouncing a sentence (Jer 48:46-47).

The miracle stories of Elijah and Elisha were told in villages
from which monarchs taxed food and recruited warriors (1 Sam
8:11-17; 1 Kgs 21:1-29). The miracles of these prophets were not
so much authorizations of their power but, rather, indictments of
the monarchs' misuse of power. Virtually all the miracles focused
on some aspect of feeding and protecting. Miracles demonstrated
the effortlessness with which Yahweh could feed and protect the
people in contrast to the costly efforts of the monarchs to feed and
protect them through covenants with other nations. For example,
monarchs took widows' sons for the army, thus putting them to
death, whereas Elisha raised the son of the widow of Zarephath to
life (1 Kgs 17:17-24). Monarchs taxed widows to death, but Elijah
gave the widow an endless supply of oil (2 Kgs 4:1-7). And when a
borrowed axe necessary to clear the land was lost, Elisha returned it
so that the lender would not foreclose on the land to pay for the
axe (1 Kgs 6:1-7).

The Prophet's   As the loyal opposition to the priestly commu-
Social Role   nity and the monarchy, prophets expressed an
                  egalitarian ideal of a society in which every
person is equal under the law. Sometimes the prophets are men-

tioned as part of the cult community (e.g., Isaiah and Ezekiel) and as court prophets (e.g., Nathan). Still, they seem always to have been able to stand apart from these institutions to criticize them and to point out where they have broken the covenant with God. In doing so, these "establishment prophets" created a following of disciples or a school of thought that preserved the message of the prophet and eventually organized it into a written, coherent document.

Occasionally a prophet such as Elijah or Elisha may appear to be totally autonomous and in fact peripheral to the mainstream of society. Even these apparently lone prophets, however, were part of a social group that functioned as a sort of underground network of material and spiritual support. This social group would have provided meals and lodging for the prophet and would also have helped him carry out his mission (see 2 Kgs 9:1–10).

In the political realm, the prophets served as the conscience of the kings. It was their job to remind the monarch that he was not above the law and could be punished like any other Israelite for an infraction of the covenant. Prophets also engaged in political acts. For instance, Elisha had one of his "sons" anoint Jehu as king (2 Kgs 9:1–13), and Jeremiah counseled King Zedekiah to surrender the city of Jerusalem to the besieging Babylonians (Jer 21:1–10; 38:17–18).

**Prophetic
Immunity**

Since the prophets were viewed as the messengers of God, they were not held liable for the message they spoke and could not be killed because of that message. But if for any reason suspicion was raised that the person was not a true prophet, then the message was to be held up to scrutiny to see whether it came true (Jer 28:8–9). Should the message prove false, then the prophet was subject to execution, either by the people or by God (compare Jer 26:12–19 and 28:16–17).

Just because a prophet was spared from death, however, did not mean that he or she would not face public ridicule and physical punishment at the hands of dissenters. For instance, the high priest Amaziah publicly denounces Amos at Bethel for speaking without license in the king's sanctuary (Amos 7:12–13).

Both Elijah and Jeremiah face public censure (1 Kgs 18:17; Jer 36:21–26), and Jeremiah is imprisoned (Jer 38:4–6) and placed in the stocks (Jer 20:2).

Concern with the Present and Near Future   Because their job was to draw the people and the establishment back to the proper covenant relationship with Yahweh, prophets were concerned about the present and the near future. Sometimes their work was conducted prior to God's punishment, and sometimes their words served as an explanation for why God had punished the people. Such an explanation is a **theodicy,** which offers reasons for why God allows evil or destruction to occur.

The major exception to the prophetic concern for the present and the near future is **apocalyptic** prophecy. By definition, apocalyptic utterance is concerned with "end things" **(eschatology)** and contains elements of tradition and history that are hidden in symbolic language. Zechariah and Daniel are the best examples of apocalyptic prophets. The portions of these books that contain this type of literature are usually dated to the latter portion of Israelite history (200 B.C.E. and later). As a result, they employ many of the ideas and themes of earlier prophets. But they speak to a future time when the problems of the present are solved and God reigns over a restored nation.

The Prophetic Theme of the Remnant   Each prophet develops the theme of a remnant. The theme reflects the belief that a righteous God cannot utterly destroy righteous persons without giving them a chance to survive. The story of Noah and the flood is an early example of this theme, although God speaks directly to Noah instead of employing a prophet (see Gen 6–9). In later Israelite history, however, it is the prophet who serves as the bearer of a message of retribution by God for the failure of the people to obey the covenant. Their punishment is certain, but a remnant may survive the coming destruction and rebuild the nation from the ashes. Ezekiel's vision of the "marking of the innocents" is one of the best examples of this message (Ezek 9). In this vision, which may be a parallel to the Passover account of Exod 12, divine messengers mark those persons who demonstrate a true repentance and sorrow over the sins of Jerusalem. When the rest of the population is executed and the city is destroyed, the ones who have been marked are spared.

The Reinterpreta- Prophetic speech has a long history of reinter-
tion of Prophecy pretation. We have already noted that proph-
ets often take up themes and imagery from earlier prophets. This process continues as the words of the prophets are collected and written down. During the Christian era, prophetic materials were used by the writers of the New Testament and later by Christian theologians as the basis of their doctrines. A famous example is Matthew's use of Isa 7:14 (Matt 1:23). These later commentaries on the words of the Hebrew prophets are not invalid, but it should not be assumed that the original intention of a particular prophet was to foretell the birth of Jesus or the establishment of Christianity.

3

PREMONARCHIC PROPHETIC ACTIVITY

While prophecy is usually considered a phenomenon of the monarchic period, prophets do appear in the biblical narrative prior to the time of Saul and David. The two most prominent of these figures are Moses and Balaam. Because so little is known about their social world, it is difficult to reconstruct how they interact with it. There is little attempt made by the biblical writers to flesh out either the Egyptian setting for Moses or the culture of the Moabites in the Balaam narrative. The principal purpose in both stories is crisis management, with a human serving as a conduit for divine power. It is clearly more important to the theology of the writers to demonstrate **Yahweh's** supremacy over other divine figures. What later readers may learn about life in Egypt, in the Sinai, or in Transjordan is not really germane to this purpose.

MOSES

Moses is obviously more than a prophet. His leadership is all-encompassing, and he functions in both secular and **cultic** capacities. He not only hears the cases of the people (Exod 18:13) but also orchestrates sacrifices (Exod 24:5–6). In addition, he is closely associated with the tent of meeting, a sacred precinct otherwise restricted to the priestly community (Exod 40).

What may be most useful here in our discussion of prophetic activity is the account of Moses' **call,** which provides the basic **framework** for the calls of several later prophets (especially Isaiah) and sets a tone for **theophanies** elsewhere in the biblical narrative. His call (Exod 3:1–4:18) may be outlined in four stages.

(1) The theophany occurs in the form of a "burning bush." This miraculous phenomenon demonstrates Yahweh's mastery over creation and forces Moses to turn aside from his own activities to pay attention to this marvelous sight. No call occurs without a divine manifestation. The theophany must include an identification of God and a reason for its occurrence.

(2) The human reacts with fear to the theophany and immediately offers a **demurral,** or excuse for why he or she should not be the one to perform the assigned task. Moses' excuses are particularly creative. In each case, God rejects the excuse. Moses says he is a nobody (true, but not a sufficient reason for excusing him). He delays by asking God's name; God responds with a theological pun based on the verbal root of Yahweh's name ("I Am Sent You"). He asks for some means of proving he is coming as a representative of God; God gives him the power to perform a series of signs. And finally, he declares that he has no training or ability to speak before audiences, much less the god-king pharaoh. This final demurral allows for the introduction of Moses' brother Aaron into the narrative.

(3) Once the human has run out of excuses, God then provides **resolution.** The deity dismisses the mortal's excuses by saying that he or she will have Yahweh's words and power working for the newly appointed prophet.

(4) No further argument is possible, and as God lays out the **mission** of the prophet, the only response can be, "Here am I, send me," or in this instance "us."

Moses' prophetic activity is demonstrated in the contest with Egypt's pharaoh and in the sequence of ten plagues. The account of the ten plagues is a literary framework that systematizes Moses' conflict with Pharaoh to demonstrate clearly to the Egyptians who Yahweh is (Exod 7:5). Each time Pharaoh refuses to allow the Israelites to go into the desert to worship Yahweh, Moses predicts the coming of a plague. Occasionally Aaron is the more active participant (Exod 8:16–17), but the sequence remains basically the same. When Pharaoh is forced to acknowledge that he and his magicians cannot end a particular plague, Moses then predicts the end of that calamity. As God manipulates Pharaoh by hardening his heart, the cycle then repeats itself, as a didactic exercise for the benefit of the Israelites (see Exod 7:14–12:51).

Plague Sequence

Moses asks Pharaoh to allow the Israelites to worship Yahweh for three days in the desert.

Yahweh "hardens Pharaoh's heart," and the king refuses to cooperate.

Moses predicts a plague.

Unable to stop the plague, Pharaoh asks Moses to pray to Yahweh to end the plague.

After the plague ends, Yahweh "hardens Pharaoh's heart" again, and the king again refuses to allow the Israelites to go worship.

Similar examples of Moses' ability to seek God's aid occur in the narratives of the wilderness wandering, when the people "murmur" over a lack of food or water (see Exod 16:1–8). The vast majority of Moses' attention, however, is given over to administrative (Exod 18:13) and military affairs (Exod 17:8–15) during the Sinai and wilderness treks. He is by no means only a prophet once the people leave Egypt.

BALAAM

The other significant prophet in the premonarchic period is Balaam. This non-Israelite seer apparently had gained a reputation as a true prophet, someone whose predictions in the name of a god came true. His name and at least one example of his prophetic ability are recorded in an eighth-century B.C.E. Aramaic inscription found at Deir 'Alla in the eastern Jordan Valley:

> This is the story of Balaam, son of Beor and a seer. The divine assembly appeared to Balaam, son of Beor, at night. He dreamed he heard El pronounce a death sentence on his city. ("Stories of Balaam," *OTP*, p. 124)

His reputation as a seer is the basis for an attempt by the king of Moab to use Balaam's powers to curse the invading Israelites (Num 22–24). Balak describes Balaam as so attuned to the gods that both his blessings and his curses are always effective. The prophet, as a god's intermediary or representative, is believed therefore to be capable of interceding for good or ill with the god(s). In the process, however, both Balaam and Balak are given a lesson on the power of God to control the speech of a prophet. As Balaam says repeatedly in his professional disclaimer, prophets may be asked to do something, but if they are true to their calling, they can only speak the words given to them by God.

> Do I have the power to say just anything? The word God puts in my mouth, that is what I must say. (Num 22:38)

Although the narrative makes Balaam the butt of a divine joke (see Num 22:22–35), it depicts him as a Yahweh prophet and is fairly sympathetic to him. Balaam does employ sacrificial rituals to obtain God's answer, but he is not simply a diviner; in fact, he abandons his usual procedure of invoking a god or seeking an omen through **divination.** Having perceived that Yahweh's intent is to bless the Israelites, he leaves himself open to direct revelation from God. At this point, he becomes empowered to speak God's blessing on the Israelites.

Later traditions treat Balaam as a pawn whose curse is transformed into a blessing by the God of the Israelites (Deut 23:5; Josh 24:9–10; Neh 13:2). This more negative appraisal of Balaam may be due to the biblical writers' desire to champion only Israelite prophets. The **universalism** theme that runs throughout much of the biblical text is present in both the positive and the negative portrayals of Balaam. In both versions, Yahweh is proven to be a powerful deity without any divine rival.

4

EARLY MONARCHIC PROPHETS

Israel is portrayed as a fairly unified people during the formative period of the exodus and conquest. The leadership of Moses and Joshua, while not unquestioned, held sway over the people and tied them together until the promised land was in their grasp. This is at least the story told by the writers of Exodus, Numbers, Deuteronomy, and Joshua. The chaos that dominates the tales in the book of Judges, however, suggests that there was little unanimity during the early years of Israel's settlement in the land. The political and social evolution of the nation required the elevation of strong national leaders as chiefs and eventually as monarchs.

SAMUEL

Given the ancient Israelite belief in a cyclical universe, it is not surprising that the reader of the biblical narrative will be continually presented with a succession of figures like Moses. During the period of transition between the time of the Judges and the beginning of monarchy, this figure is Samuel. Like Elijah in a later period, he will share many characteristics with Moses, including the following.

(1) **Miraculous circumstances at birth.** Moses barely survived Pharaoh's order to exterminate the Hebrew male infants (Exod 2;1–10). Samuel was born after his mother had been barren for years and become pregnant only through divine intervention.

(2) **Call.** Although Samuel's **call** occurred when he was a child (1 Sam 3), it involved a **theophany,** an amusing byplay of mistaken identity, and an acceptance of the task by what would otherwise be considered an unlikely candidate.

(3) **Military success.** Like Moses, Samuel led the Israelites to victory against their enemies. For both Moses and Samuel, this victory was accomplished with the aid of **Yahweh,** the **Divine Warrior** (1 Sam 7:7–11; see Exod 16:8–13).

(4) **Judge over the people.** Like Moses, Samuel heard the legal complaints of the Israelites (1 Sam 7:15–17; Exod 18:13). During the period of the Judges, Deborah also functioned in a judicial capacity. Unlike Samuel, however, Deborah's story centers on a single episode and does not describe her career in detail (Judg 4–5).

In addition to these characteristics, which resemble Moses' leadership, Samuel also had a great reputation as a seer. In the latter capacity, he could be consulted on any matter of concern to the people, whether public or private. The situation of the people during this transitional period may have required that Samuel perform a variety of roles. There was, for example, neither a central government nor a central shrine where governors or priests could serve all of the tribes. Even Samuel exerted his authority over only a small area in the central region of Palestine's hill country. This area was a circuit of cities ranging from the **cultic** sites at Bethel, Gilgal, and Mizpah to his own hometown of Ramah. Still, with the possible exception of Deborah, Samuel's authority stretched over more territory than the other judges were able to control.

Even with these limitations, however, Samuel provided a pattern of authority that had not existed since the time of Joshua. Getting the people to look to a central authority figure was crucial as the tribes emerged from their fiercely held local autonomy to forge a chiefdom led by Saul and his supporters. It was no small thing for the tribes to relinquish their individual control over their armed forces and allow a combined army to be commanded by a figure who did not belong to their tribe or clan. Such a situation is admirably portrayed in the ancient "Song of Deborah," which condemns several tribes who refused to join forces even during a time of great crisis (Judg 5:13–18). Perhaps because he was widely regarded as a divine intermediary, Samuel facilitated the transition to statehood. When the tribes of Israel faced a crisis that required the cooperation of more than two or three tribes, they could turn to the prophet Samuel.

It is in fact Samuel's reputation as a seer that brings the young Saul to him (see 1 Sam 9:9). Although the meeting is ostensibly about a private matter, it also inaugurates an entirely new political and religious arrangement in Israel. It also creates a new role for prophets, who will be involved in the selection of kings and also serve as their chief critics from this point on.

In this early period, the roles and responsibilities of both the kings and the prophets had to be carefully worked out; and, not surprisingly, the process of defining these separate roles involved considerable conflict. The conflict is described in a series of narratives beginning with Samuel's anointing of Saul with oil. The act of anointing with oil is significant in at least two ways (10:1). First, not only does it designate God's choice, it also reminds the king of the importance of the prophet who has anointed him. Second, because olive oil was involved in nearly every aspect of life, it serves as a perfect symbol of the many responsibilities of the monarch for the lives of his people.

Once Saul became king, he quickly discovered that his word was not absolute and that he must continue to bow not only to God's command but also to the directives of God's representative, Samuel. It must have galled the man who had "danced with the prophets" and prophesied himself (10:10–13) to be forced to limit his actions when he knew what needed to be done. The narrative emphatically demonstrates, however, that the king is not above either the law or God's representative.

The prime example of the tension between Samuel and Saul occurs when Saul must act in his role as military chief. The issue is whether Saul will carry out this role in obedience to Yahweh, Israel's Divine Warrior, or whether he will act on his own. The tension is played out as Saul waits for Samuel to appear at Gilgal. As he waits the requisite seven days, the Philistines gather in strength, and the Israelite warriors begin to slip away. When Samuel does not appear, Saul takes matters into his own hands and offers a sacrifice to God before going into battle with the Philistines. Perhaps his sacrifice was a way of calling on God for help, or perhaps it was to determine if Yahweh would be with him in battle. Neither reason adequately accounted for his actions, though, because he was only supposed to wait for Samuel to arrive. Samuel reminds Saul that patience is not a luxury for military or political leaders; rather, it is a necessity for those who would trust in God. By taking matters into his own hands, Saul has not only usurped Samuel's role as diviner, he has also proven his lack of faith in God's ability to help Israel (13:8–14).

When Samuel gives him another chance to demonstrate his loyalty to Yahweh, Saul fails again. In the name of Yahweh, Samuel calls on Saul to conduct a *herem,* or holy war, against the Amalekites, an Israelite enemy since Moses' time (Exod 17:8–16). In effect, Samuel expects Saul to continue the war of conquest begun by Joshua, since the *herem* is a form of ethnic cleansing that will rid Israel of a perennial enemy and cultural threat. The king does slaughter the Amalekites in battle, but he does not completely obey Samuel. Instead he takes rich spoils back with him to his capital to demonstrate his prowess.

The situation is ripe for confrontation, and Samuel does not disappoint us. The rich sarcasm and doomsaying are a forerunner of prophetic speech during the divided monarchy. Saul tries to excuse himself by claiming that the people took a portion of the spoil as a sacrifice to God. This cannot justify, however, his failure to obey the divine command.

> What is this bleating of sheep in my ears, and the lowing of cattle that I hear? . . . The LORD anointed you king over Israel. And the LORD sent you on a mission. . . . Why then did you not obey the voice of the LORD? (1 Sam 15:14, 17–19)

The simple answer is that Saul has disobeyed again, and this pattern of disobedience now causes God to reconsider the claim of Saul's family to the throne. Some of this narrative obviously has been reworked to suit the needs of the Davidic dynasty, since Samuel's announcement that God "has torn the kingdom of Israel from you this very day" (15:28) adds authority and legitimacy to David's claim to the monarchy. The statement in 15:22–23, which is less obviously tinged with Davidic political interests, articulates a general theological principle:

> Has the LORD as great delight in burnt offerings and sacrifices,
> as in obeying the voice of the LORD? Surely, to obey is better
> than sacrifice, and to heed than the fat of rams. (v. 22)

This statement of what is expected of all kings becomes a ready cliché in later prophetic speech (compare Hos 6:6). In this confrontation, the prophet as Yahweh's representative must win out over the king. God can anoint someone king, but this king must in turn provide an example of both leadership and obedience to the nation. Otherwise the prophet is waiting in the wings to choose a new king at God's command. At least, this is the principle until the establishment of the hereditary monarchy, when a new relationship must be initiated to keep the kings in check.

In any case, God instructs Samuel to seek out a more suitable candidate to replace the house of Saul on the throne (1 Sam 16:1–13). The somewhat comical narrative in which David is anointed points up the fact that prophets are human and therefore capable of error. Samuel is very impressed with Jesse's older sons but eventually must ask the old man if he has any other sons, since God has not been as impressed with them as the prophet has been. David, the younger son, will then take Saul's place as the "Lord's anointed" and will spend many years growing into a job he cannot ascend to until Saul's death. The entire narrative is part of the "apology of David," which disqualifies Saul's descendants from inheriting Saul's throne and promotes the establishment of the Davidic monarchy.

One final prophetic role played by Samuel occurs after his death. In the final days of his rule, Saul is completely cut off from God. Samuel is dead, no other prophetic or priestly voice has taken Samuel's place, and most poignantly, God no longer speaks directly to Saul (contrast 10:10–11; 19:19–24). Faced with an imminent battle with the militarily superior Philistines, Saul illegally consults the Witch of Endor and asks her to conjure up the ghost of Samuel so he may ask him about the future (28:3–25). Samuel's response is predictable. He simply repeats in summary fashion all of his previous statements, condemning Saul for his disobedient actions. The ghostly prophet then predicts the king's demise along with his sons. This narrative makes clear that prophets are not gods to be consulted through mediums and wizards. They function only as spokespersons for God, and they do not take the initiative to speak in their own name.

NATHAN

When David comes to power, he must further solidify his position against tribal fragmentation. He does this by establishing himself as a strong military leader, by capturing Jerusalem and making it his royal capital, and by placing the **ark of the covenant** in Jerusalem. This last act ties the secular and sacred authority to that place and also associates it with his rule. In the midst of this consolidation of royal power, the prophet Nathan will both build up and tear down David's royal ego.

The prophet Nathan is depicted as a member of David's royal court. One might expect that, as such, he would be a loyalist. This certainly seems to be the case when he announces that God intends to establish an everlasting **covenant** with David and his descendants. The context of the **oracle** is that David has expressed a desire to build a "house" or temple for Yahweh. While Nathan's oracle appears at first to be a rejection of David's efforts to confine Yahweh to a "house," it becomes instead a divine promise to establish an everlasting dynasty. By playing on the meaning of the word "house," Nathan proclaims that David will not build a "house" or temple for God; instead God will build a "house" or "dynasty" for David (2 Sam 7:8–17).

God's promise of an everlasting dynasty establishes a covenant relationship with David that not only legitimates David's authority to succeed Saul on the throne; it also sanctions a hereditary monarchy. Such a divine promise does not, however, give the kings a blank check to use their power in any way they please. Nathan's oracle affirms that kings must still obey God's commands. Individual kings can and will be punished for their sins; nevertheless, God will remain loyal to his promise to David to establish his dynasty. Thus the oracle concludes with the observation that what happened to Saul and his family will not happen to David's.

This new relationship between God and the king also has an impact on the relationship between the prophet and the king. When David sins by engaging in an adulterous affair with Bathsheba and then arranging for the death of her husband, Uriah, to cover up the affair (2 Sam 11), it is Nathan who announces God's judgment of David. Nathan employs a juridical parable that forces David to acknowledge his guilt and pronounce his own punishment:

> There were two men in a certain city, the one rich and the other poor. The rich man had very many flocks and herds; but the poor man had nothing but one little ewe lamb, which he had bought. He brought it up, and it grew up with him and with his children; it used to eat of his meager fare, and drink from his cup, and lie in his bosom, and it was like a daughter to him. Now there came a traveler to the rich man, and he was loath to take one of his own flock or herd to prepare for the wayfarer who had come to him, but he took the poor man's lamb, and prepared that for the guest who had come to him. (12:1–4)

Note the points of this transparent parable. There is a power difference between the men, based on wealth. The poor man has a single possession, other than his family, that he values. The rich man violates the laws of hospitality by taking the lamb from the poor man instead of taking an animal from his own flock. All of these statements are an obvious indictment, as they graphically illustrate what David has done by taking Uriah's wife, Bathsheba. Thus Nathan can charge David without naming him until David has passed judgment on the "rich man" (12:5–7).

Adultery is a capital crime (Deut 22:22), but a conviction requires two witnesses (Deut 19:15). In this case only God is a witness, but since it is the king who has committed the crime, there must be a recompense to fit the crime. Nathan's parable forces David to acknowledge his behavior, to confess and repent (2 Sam 12:12–13). Although his dynasty will not be abolished as Saul's was, the child of adultery will die (12:14), and David will have to face the anguish of rebellion and dissension within his own house (12:10–11).

Nathan's use of the parable of the ewe lamb is an example of the **motif** of the king's call to justice (see also 1 Kgs 21:17–29). When the king violates the covenant, a prophet or other divine representative confronts him. If the king confesses and repents, his punishment is passed to the next generation.

This literary motif depicts the prophet administering justice on the highest-ranking member of Israelite society. Through the use of the parable, the prophet requires that the king acknowledge that Yahweh can discern what might otherwise be hidden to human investigators. Thus the prophet becomes the champion of the covenant as well as the voice of God sitting in judgment.

AHIJAH

There must have been some consternation on the part of the biblical writers when they were faced with the division of the kingdom after the reign of Solomon. A great deal of effort had gone into creating an **apology,** or justification, for David's assumption of power. Solomon had been portrayed as a wise king who could create a general prosperity throughout the land, construct a magnificent temple of Yahweh, and strengthen the bonds of unity within the nation. The reality of Israel's political divisions becomes evident in the reaction to Solomon's policy of diplomatic marriages. Having many wives was not the issue. Instead it was the construction of shrines to the gods of his foreign wives that required a divine reaction and a stern admonition from the prophet Ahijah (1 Kgs 11:9–13). The covenant that had been made with David was not to be set aside, but as part of Solomon's punishment, his son Rehoboam would lose control over all but the southern portion of the kingdom.

Ahijah's task is modeled after that of Samuel in 1 Sam 16:1–13, when he went in search of Saul's successor and rival. God has determined that the nation will be divided and a new king must be found for the northern nation. Thus Ahijah seeks out Jeroboam, a member of Solomon's bureaucracy and therefore a man with some administrative experience (1 Kgs 11:28). Instead of anointing him, however, Ahijah performs a very different symbolic act. Taking his new garment, Ahijah tears it into twelve pieces. He instructs Jeroboam to take ten of these strips of cloth as his assurance that he will rule the ten northern tribes of Israel. Only one tribe is to be retained by Solomon's son Rehoboam as a sign of the continuation of the Davidic covenant (11:29–37).

Ahijah's oracle establishes two separate tracks to the monarchy. The Davidic covenant provides for the divinely sanctioned, hereditary monarchy in the southern kingdom. There will be a continuous line of Davidic kings in Judah until the fall of Jerusalem in 587 B.C.E. This will not be a trouble-free dynasty, but only two monarchs will be assassinated, and there will be no break or change of ruling families. The relationship between God and the kings in the north, however, reverts back to the "monarch on trial" arrangement that had been employed during Saul's rule. Each one of these northern kings will be presented with the obligation to uphold the terms of the covenant, and each will be expected to obey it without wavering. Thus God says to Jeroboam:

> If you will listen to all that I command you, walk in my ways, and do what is right in my sight by keeping my statutes and my commandments, as David my servant did, I will be with you, and will build you an enduring house, as I built for David, and I will give Israel to you. (11:38)

According to the Judean narrators of 1–2 Kings, the kings of Israel were never able to meet this very strict standard of behavior. Jeroboam himself sets the tone for misrule by committing what these writers call the **"sins of Jeroboam."** These writers maintain that Jeroboam sinned because he established cultic centers at Dan and Bethel, placed golden calves in the shrines at Dan and Bethel as a substitute for the ark of the covenant, created a non-Levitical priesthood, changed the religious calendar, and encouraged the use of local **"high places."**

Although the Judean writers label these actions as sin, we can also understand them as strategies designed to create political autonomy for the northern kingdom. For example, the sanctuaries at Dan and Bethel were intended to prevent Israelite travel to Jerusalem (1 Kgs 12:28–33). Still, Jeroboam's politically motivated decrees become the criteria that will be used by the biblical writers to judge the actions of all future kings. Thus a just king is one who obeys the covenant and a bad king is one who continues the sins of Jeroboam. Naturally, after such horrendous monarchic sins, Ahijah will be obliged to condemn Jeroboam, just as Samuel had to reject Saul. Worst of all, his family also will be denied the chance to establish itself as dynasts in Israel (14:6–14). Thereafter the succession to the throne is governed more by military power than by legal rights. In the northern kingdom, succession by assassination becomes the rule rather than the exception.

THE UNNAMED "MAN OF GOD" FROM JUDAH

One further point to be made about Jeroboam involves an unnamed "man of God" from Judah, who confronts the new king during the inauguration ceremony of the king's newly built royal shrine at Bethel. It is curious that Ahijah is not the one to stand before the triumphant king at Bethel and condemn him for his hubris. Since the narrative also contains the prophecy of the coming of Josiah and the destruction of Bethel's altar in the late seventh century B.C.E. (1 Kgs 13:2–3), however, it is quite likely that this story represents a separate tradition from the Ahijah narrative. The episode suggests that Jeroboam's "sins" begin when he establishes an illegitimate shrine, separate from Jerusalem.

The narrative is also concerned with the nature of royal and prophetic authority. The prophet completely ignores Jeroboam and directs his curse against Bethel and its altar; this deliberate snub of Jeroboam suggests that God has already revoked Jeroboam's authority to rule. When the prophet refuses Jeroboam's offer of hospitality, he again reiterates his lack of respect for the king. This episode also sets up the second part of the narrative, in which the prophet's obedience is tested.

The narrative also illustrates the principle of **prophetic immunity.** When prophets perform their divinely ordained task, it is assumed that the God they represent protects them. As a result, when Jeroboam stretches out his hand and gestures to have the prophet arrested, he is afflicted with a withered arm and the altar is destroyed. The king is duly frightened by this display of divine power and begs for the man of God to intercede for him (13:4–6). The man of God does this, and Jeroboam is promptly healed.

The curious story in the second half of the narrative (13:11–32) is another demonstration that no one, not even a prophet, may disobey God's command without being punished (see also Num 20:1–13). The man of God has been told not to turn aside or return home by the same path (1 Kgs 13:17). An old prophet of Bethel assures him, however, that he has received an angelic message giving the other man license to stop for a meal (13:18). Lack of faith in his original instructions becomes the basis for the death of the man of God and his burial in a strange tomb (13:24–32). The Bethel prophet's story serves as an early example of **cognitive dissonance,** in which two seemingly truthful statements are in direct conflict. The moral of the story, as in many of the tales in which prophets confront kings, is that strict obedience to God's command is the highest imperative in life.

Jezebel for Ahab's failures. While such a marriage would have established a logical political alliance between Israel and Phoenicia, the biblical writers present it as an invasion by the forces of Baal religion. Jezebel's name becomes synonymous with wickedness and infidelity. She hunts down the prophets and worshipers of **Yahweh,** killing all she can find. In the meantime, Ahab does nothing to stop her.

ELIJAH CYCLE

Elijah and Elisha are the heroes of this story. They are portrayed as larger than life, and their actions for good and evil are magnified in the text. Elijah bursts on the scene without so much as a formal story of his **call** or even an introduction. He confronts the powers of state and temple and predicts a three-year drought and famine throughout the land of Israel (17:1). Because Jezebel's god Baal was believed to be a god of storms and fertility, Elijah's prophecy directly challenges Baal's power and asserts that it is Yahweh who controls the rains and harvests. The theme of this prophet and all others is firmly set forth: "Who really is God?"

Elijah spends the three years of the drought east of the Jordan River and also in Phoenicia at Zarephath (17:2–24). By performing life-giving miracles during this time, he demonstrates the power of his God, whose **covenant** promise was to provide land and children. Elijah provides food to a starving widow and her son. Then, after the son has apparently died, he revives the son. Elijah's actions stand in stark contrast to those of Ahab and Jezebel, who take away life with their purge of Yahweh worshipers and who, by their introduction of the worship of Baal, are the cause of the famine in the land.

Contest on Mount Carmel   When the initial testing period is over, God instructs Elijah to return to Israel and challenge Ahab to a contest that will dramatically demonstrate Yahweh's power and Baal's impotence (1 Kgs 18). Not since Moses' time has there been such a direct, public confronta-

5

ELIJAH AND ELISHA

In the period immediately after the division of the kingdo
no strong prophetic figure emerges. As we have seen above, tꞏ
prophets condemn Jeroboam in two separate incidents (1 ꞏ
11:9–13; 13:1–10); but these are apparently isolated events that
not represent a systematic effort at reform. Not until the ninth cꞏ
tury will prophets appear who will be able to launch an effect
challenge against the king and the religious establishment in ꞏ
northern kingdom. These prophets are Elijah and Elisha.

This is a shadowy time in Israelite history. Other than
biblical narrative, what is known comes from the records of
Assyrian king Shalmaneser III (858–824 B.C.E.). On his "Monoli
inscription, Shalmaneser records his official version of the battle
Qarqar on the Orontes River in Syria in 853 B.C.E. Among the pꞏ
rulers mustered against him was Ahab, king of Israel, who is saiꞏ
have supplied two thousand chariots and ten thousand soldi
Such numbers suggest that Ahab was among the leaders of
coalition and a relatively powerful and influential ruler.

This is not the biblical picture of Ahab. In 1 Kings, he and
Phoenician wife, Jezebel, are portrayed as villains. Furthermꞏ
Ahab hardly appears as a powerful ruler, since he is comple
dominated by his strong-willed wife. In fact, the narrator blaꞏ

tion between a king/leader and a prophet. But while Moses challenged a foreign king, the pharaoh of Egypt, Elijah's confrontation is with an Israelite king.

The site for the trial is Mount Carmel, which overlooks the Mediterranean coast and would serve as a perfect platform from which to watch for storms coming in from the sea. The rules of the contest are quite simple. Elijah and the four hundred prophets of Baal each construct an altar. The Baal prophets and then Elijah call upon their god in turn to accept the sacrificial bull. The gods would indicate their acceptance of the sacrifice by casting down divine fire upon the altar and bringing rain to end the drought. The suspense, as well as the comic nature of this story, is heightened when Elijah lets the opposition go first. Their daylong pleading with Baal goes unanswered despite their "limping" dance and ritual bloodletting (18:26–28). These acts may be part of a mourning ritual (see Deut 14:1), but more likely they are designed to invoke a storm god during the summer months, when he would ordinarily be absent in the underworld. Elijah taunts their failed performance and ridicules their nonresponsive god:

> Cry aloud! Surely he is a god; either he is meditating, or he has wandered away, or he is on a journey, or perhaps he is asleep and must be awakened. (1 Kgs 18:27)

Elijah's taunt takes its cue from Ugaritic epic literature. In the Baal cycle, Baal embarks on long journeys, much like Gilgamesh of ancient Mesopotamia or Hercules of ancient Greece. In addition, the idea that he was sleeping may have been part of the ritual of awakening associated with the rains that ended summer droughts each year. Admittedly, the references to meditating or wandering away are more profane and probably refer to the practice of defecating in a field (see Gen 24:63).

Elijah takes his turn next and performs a series of symbolic acts designed to restore Yahweh as the God of Israel (1 Kgs 18:30–40). He gathers the people around him and rebuilds the platform of a ruined altar that was previously dedicated to Yahweh (compare Judg 6:28–32). He then takes twelve stones representing the twelve tribes of Israel and uses them to build an altar in Yahweh's name (compare Josh 4:1–9). Finally, he digs a trench around the altar and has water poured over the sacrificial bull and wood three times, thus filling the trench and saturating the fuel for the sacrifice. This last step symbolizes the bounty of the coming rain and, in addition, will demonstrate that no chance spark will ignite his sacrifice.

Then at a time specifically appointed during the day for sacrifices and oblations (1 Kgs 18:29), Elijah calls upon Yahweh to demonstrate that the "God of Abraham, Isaac, and Israel" is "God in Israel" and that Elijah is his prophet. This parallels the account of Moses' confrontation with Pharaoh and suggests just how closely the biblical writers patterned the Elijah cycle after the Moses narratives. Yahweh's response is immediate. No elaborate ritual acts are necessary, and there is no opportunity for Baal's priests to taunt Elijah or God. The sacrifice, the altar, and the water are all consumed by divine fire from heaven.

Such a decisive act elicits two powerful emotions on the part of Elijah's audience. First, in the face of **theophanic** manifestation, they are afraid, and this causes them to make a statement of abject submission, "The LORD indeed is God!" (18:39). Then, perhaps as an emotional release, the people become fiercely angry. Responding to Elijah's command, they massacre the prophets of Baal (18:40); perhaps this part of the story reflects the Deuteronomic command to slay false prophets (Deut 13:1–5). Finally, after Elijah's servant performs a sevenfold ritual, it begins to rain (1 Kgs 18:41–46).

Elijah's Theophany on Mount Horeb Even though Elijah has won the contest and demonstrated the superiority of Yahweh's power to Baal's, Jezebel remains a formidable opponent. When she threatens to kill Elijah, he runs away in fear of his life (19:2). The fact that Elijah has operated to this point as an outsider now works against him. As a Gileadite from the area east of the Jordan River, he has no ties to any group or person other than a servant, and apparently he has no strong clan ties or political power base in Israel. His flight may reflect this lack of crucial support. Since so much of the Elijah narrative appears to have been modeled after the events of Moses' life, however, it may simply be the case that Elijah's flight was patterned to resemble Moses' initial flight from Egypt (Exod 2:11–15; see also Exod 12). Just as Moses fled Egypt and journeyed to Mount Sinai, so also will Elijah journey to Mount Horeb (since Mount Sinai is called Mount Horeb in these narratives, the destination of Moses and Elijah is the same). While he is in the wilderness, Elijah must rely on God to feed him, just as the Israelites did. He survives his journey to Mount Horeb only because an angel provides bread and water (1 Kgs 19:4–8; compare Exod 16).

When Elijah arrives at Mount Horeb, he will receive his call, which is absent from the earlier narrative. The call is staged like other divine encounters with fugitives (see Gen 16:7–12). God asks him, "What are you doing here, Elijah?" In response to such a question, a fugitive generally produces an excuse or a justification, and Elijah does both. He explains that he has been working zealously for Yahweh but that he has now taken flight so that there will be at least one voice left to defend God.

The ensuing theophany is mystifying. Elijah experiences strong winds, earthquake, and fire. All of these are typical manifestations of Yahweh's power, and they are frequently found in biblical accounts of theophanies. But the narrator emphasizes that none of these—earthquake, wind, or fire—contains the spirit of God. Instead the prophet perceives the presence of Yahweh only in the silence that follows these manifestations (1 Kgs 19:11–13). The narrator may be drawing a clear distinction between Yahweh and Baal, a storm god whose theophanies would also be characterized by earthquake, wind, and fire. It is also possible that the theophany has been reshaped by a later writer whose theology has moved beyond simple natural events as signs for God and who now wishes to show that Yahweh's presence is both universal and internal. In any case, after the theophany, Yahweh again asks Elijah why he has come to Mount Horeb. Yahweh then charges the prophet to perform three acts that will transform Israel religiously and politically (19:15–16). First, he is to anoint Hazael as king of Aram (Syria). Second, he is to anoint Jehu as king over Israel. Finally, he is to anoint Elisha as his prophetic successor.

Elijah performs only the third task and leaves the first two for Elisha, whom he designates as his successor by **casting his mantle** over Elisha's shoulders. In much the same way that Moses uses his staff to open the Red Sea (Exod 14:16), Elijah and Elisha later will use this mantle as an object of power to open up the Jordan River

(2 Kgs 2:8). Requesting and receiving permission to say good-bye to his parents (contrast Luke 9:61–62), Elisha then disappears from the narrative until 2 Kgs 1.

Naboth and the   The cycle of stories about Elijah resumes in
King's Call to   1 Kgs 21 with the story of Naboth's vineyard.
Justice   This narrative is a classic example of the **motif**
of the king's call to justice, which addresses two questions: What are the qualities of a just king? What recourse do the people have when a king abuses his power?

King Ahab wishes to add Naboth's fine vineyard to his own property. But Naboth resists this offer and exercises his rights to refuse either to sell or exchange his land for another field. His case is based on the principle that ownership and inheritance of the land is tied to Yahweh's covenant promise. Naboth believes that he will be depriving his sons of their inheritance in the covenant community if he releases ownership of his original bequest. Ahab has no recourse under law and must accept his failure in this case.

Jezebel has no such legal qualms when it comes to the exercise of royal powers. The narrators highlight the difference between Phoenician and Israelite royalty by showing that she obtains the land for her husband through deceit and force. The queen hires two false witnesses and has Naboth charged with treason and blasphemy. When Naboth is executed (along with his family, according to 2 Kgs 9:26), the land is left without an heir, and Ahab is then able to claim it as part of the royal domain.

The justice motif dominates the conclusion of the narrative. Ahab is strolling through his new property, enjoying the thrill of walking to each boundary marker of the parcel of land. Elijah confronts him there with his sin and condemns Ahab's family to a terrible fate. Not only will they suffer the loss of the throne; they will also be utterly destroyed and suffer the dishonor of being consumed by animals like so much garbage (1 Kgs 21:17–24; compare 14:7–14). The king is terrified by Elijah's curse and performs an act of contrition so complete that even Yahweh remarks on it: "Have you seen how Ahab has humbled himself before me?" In the face of the king's repentance, it would be difficult to carry out immediately God's sentence against him. The narrative ends with God declaring that the sentence will pass to Ahab's descendants, who presumably will continue to violate the covenant with God.

MICAIAH AND THE TWO KINGS

The next story, in 1 Kgs 22, describes Ahab's death in battle. The story contains all of the chilling aspects of Elijah's curse, including the motif of being consumed by animals as dogs lick up Ahab's blood. Since 1 Kgs 21 concluded that Ahab would *not* die such a horrible death, this next chapter seems contradictory. The apparent contradiction reflects a common solution employed by the editors, who evidently were well acquainted with conflicting traditions about the kings of Israel. Rather than resolve the inconsistencies by omitting this second narrative, they chose to include both stories. The narrators were therefore able to make two different theological points. The first story now illustrates God's mercy to those who truly repent, and the second demonstrates that no king is above the law.

The episode in 1 Kgs 22 introduces Micaiah as the prophet "who never prophesies anything favorable" about Ahab. The situation is a common one. Before going into battle, the kings consult either priests or prophets to determine if the **Divine Warrior** will aid them in gaining a victory (see 1 Sam 13:12). King Jehoshaphat of Judah, however, is not content to consult Ahab's four hundred court prophets, who may be biased toward their employer. As an ally, he asks for a more neutral prophetic voice, and Ahab has no choice but to grant the request.

The lone prophet Micaiah delivers a radically different message from that of Ahab's court prophets. He sees Israel scattered, "like sheep without a shepherd" (1 Kgs 22:17); his vision thus implies that Israel will lose the battle and Ahab will die. When Ahab challenges his prophecy, Micaiah reveals another vision: he has seen Yahweh put a "lying spirit" into Ahab's prophets so that they will entice him into battle, where he will die (22:19–23).

Of course, Ahab does not accept Micaiah's message. The lone prophet faces ridicule, a vast array of symbols of power, and staged demonstrations by Ahab's court prophets. Once Micaiah has spoken, the kings are faced with the problem of whom to believe. Together the court prophets' message of encouragement and Micaiah's negative one create **cognitive dissonance.** The truth can only be determined by the outcome of the battle. Ahab tries to tip the odds in his favor by imprisoning Micaiah and then disguising himself as a common soldier. This fails, of course, and dogs lap up Ahab's lifeblood as it drips from the floor of his chariot (1 Kgs 22:29–38). The exact words of Elijah's curse are fulfilled (21:19), and the prophet's authority is further enhanced.

Symbols of Power

"Now the *king* of Israel and King Jehoshaphat of Judah were sitting on their *thrones*, arrayed in their *robes*, at the *threshing floor* at the entrance of the *gate* of *Samaria*; all the *prophets* were prophesying before them" (1 Kgs 22:10–11; italics added).

Two kings represent the power of two sovereign nations.

Thrones of office symbolize their power and status.

Robes of offices mark them as kings and invest them with authority.

A threshing floor is associated with the harvest and the dispensing of justice in the village setting (Ruth 3:3–14; 2 Sam 24:18–24).

In the urban culture, the entrance of a gate is a place for business and the transaction of legal matters (Gen 19:1; Deut 21:19).

Samaria is the capital city of Israel and the symbol of its political leadership over other cities.

The court prophets of Ahab have already predicted victory for the kings, and their overwhelming numbers at this audience reinforce their authority and confidence in their message.

TRANSITION AND THE ELISHA CYCLE

Completing this cycle of Elijah stories is a short episode in which he continues to condemn Ahab's family for trusting in every god except Yahweh (2 Kgs 1:3–16). King Amaziah's decision to consult Baal-zebub of Ekron about his recovery from a fall is typical of the times (see 2 Kgs 8:7–8). Any god or divine representative who has a reputation for healing is worth consulting (compare 2 Kgs 5), but this is not appropriate for a member of Yahweh's covenant community. Later prophets will repeat Elijah's complaint against the king:

> Now if people say to you, "Consult the ghosts and the familiar spirits that chirp and mutter; should not a people consult their gods, the dead on behalf of the living, for teaching and for instruction?" Surely, those who speak like this will have no dawn! (Isa 8:19–20)

> My people consult a piece of wood, and their divining rod gives them oracles. (Hos 4:12)

A parallel theme is tied in to the judgment of Ahab's son Amaziah for his idolatry: the necessity of showing respect to a prophet as the messenger of God. The king's attempts to arrest Elijah result in the destruction of two squadrons of his soldiers at the word of the prophet (2 Kgs 1:9–12). Only when the third military commander falls on his knees and humbly approaches the prophet does Elijah consent to speak to him and prophesy for the king (1:13–16). The narrative thus sets a precedent in future dealings between king and prophet by linking respect for the prophet with respect for God.

The story of Elijah's translation to heaven marks him one last time as the successor to Moses (2:1–14). Elijah departs as mysteriously as he arrived. The traditions that surround Elijah and the fact that he is only one of two persons in the OT/HB who do not die have made him unique (the other person is Enoch; see Gen 5:24). He reappears with Moses in the story of Jesus' transfiguration in Matt 17:3–4. In later Judaism he becomes the symbol of the coming **Messiah,** and an empty chair and a glass of wine are always left for him at the Passover celebration in expectation of his return.

Following Elijah's mysterious departure, Elisha immediately takes up his master's mantle and assumes his responsibilities as the champion of Yahweh and as the chief critic of Israel's monarchy. There is a more personal character to the stories involving Elisha. In many of these stories, he helps members of Israelite society or his own group of supporters, the **sons of the prophet** or their dependents. There is less real narrative flow in the Elisha cycle than in the Elijah material, and this is probably because the editors simply grouped the stories together without concern for chronology or story line. Elisha seems to perform one miracle after another. In only a few of the stories does he confront the kings and priests; instead he is frequently portrayed as helping or encouraging the people of the land. Since the narrators have focused primarily on the deeds of the kings, their inclusion of the Elisha stories is unusual and once again highlights the Israelite **egalitarian** ideal.

The Israelite Egalitarian Ideal

Yahweh chose Israel from among all the other nations and made the covenant promise to every Israelite. Yahweh is described as "God of gods and Lord of lords . . . who is not partial and takes no bribe, who executes justice for the orphan and the widow, and who loves the strangers, providing them food and clothing" (Deut 10:17–18). Although status differences existed among the people, they all were expected to care for each other's needs, just as their God, Yahweh, did. In addition, all were to be treated equally under the law. The prophets champion this ideal as the means of obeying the covenant with Yahweh:

If you truly act justly one with another, if you do not oppress the alien, the orphan, and the widow, or shed innocent blood in this place, and if you do not go after other gods to your own hurt, then I will dwell with you in this place, in the land that I gave of old to your ancestors forever and ever. (Jer 7:5–7)

Thus says the LORD of hosts: Render true judgments, show kindness and mercy to one another; do not oppress the widow, the orphan, the alien, or the poor; and do not devise evil in your hearts against one another. (Zech 7:9–10)

The narrator's depiction of Elisha's concern to reward and protect his supporters (especially in 2 Kgs 4; 6:1–7) is a conscious attempt to demonstrate that Yahweh and his prophets will care for the faithful. Elijah's intercession for a barren couple, provision of a miraculous meal, and retrieval of a lost tool all speak to this concern for the common people.

ELISHA'S POLITICAL ROLE

In the few narratives where Elisha deals with political matters, he acts as a catalyst for judgments that Elijah announced earlier (see 1 Kgs 19:15–18). He travels to Syria and tells Hazael, a Syrian general, that he will become the new king of that country (2 Kgs 8:7–15). Later, Elisha sends one of the sons of the prophet to anoint the Israelite general Jehu as Yahweh's chosen king (9:1–10). The result of these actions is war and murder. Hazael suffocates King Ben-hadad and takes his place as the ruler of Syria (Aram). Jehu's anointing leads to the assassination of reigning kings in both Israel and Judah (8:15). The resulting civil war in Israel ends in a general purge of Ahab's family. The story reaches its climax when Jezebel attempts to thwart Jehu's efforts by labeling Jehu a "Zimri," a man who betrays his king (compare 1 Kgs 16:15–20). Jehu easily deflects her attempt by crying out, "Who is on my side?" Jehu's question forces the people to choose between himself and the house of Ahab. They choose him and throw Jezebel from a window as he rides triumphantly into Samaria (2 Kgs 9:30–37).

Labeling Techniques

Labeling can be used to honor or shame an individual or group. For a label to be effective, it must be culturally recognizable. Accepted labels become permanent and the basis for an individual's identity. These labels can, however, be accepted or rejected. To reject or deflect a label, one must either change one's behavior or appearance or provide a convincing argument that transforms public opinion.

As the new king, Jehu, garners support, persons associated with Ahab's family and the worshipers of Baal are massacred (2 Kgs 9:14–10:27). Jehu further strengthens his position by forging an alliance with Shalmaneser III of Assyria. Although this alliance is not mentioned in the biblical account, it is recorded on Shalmaneser's Black Obelisk inscription (841 B.C.E.), which includes the terms of a vassal **treaty** and portrays Jehu bowing down before the majesty of the Assyrian ruler.

Only in the story of the campaign against Moab does Elisha assume the role of a condemning prophet (2 Kgs 3). Here he travels with the combined armies of Jehoram, the son of Ahab, and Jehoshaphat, the king of Judah. It was not uncommon for priests and prophets to accompany the army, and they could interpret omens or seek divine intercession before and during battle (see Judg 4:8–9). When the expedition's ill-conceived line of march takes the combined forces into arid country that cannot support the needs of the army, the prophet is called on to save them. Elisha is reluctant to act, but because the righteous king Jehoshaphat is present, he feels a moral obligation to provide assistance. The prophet calls for a musician and subsequently enters a trance state. He then predicts that the dry wadi bed will be filled with life-giving water from rain upstream and that the expedition will ultimately be successful (2 Kgs 3:13–20).

The Moabite version of the battle appears on the Stele of Mesha, which was written for the king of Moab mentioned in 2 Kgs 3:4. Interestingly, this inscription describes complete victory for Moab. Neither the prophet Elisha nor Mesha's desperate sacrifice of his son (2 Kgs 3:26–27) is mentioned in the Moabite version of the campaign:

> I defeated the son of Omri and drove Israel out of our land forever. Omri and his son ruled the Madaba plains for forty years, but Chemosh dwells there in my time. ("Annals of Mesha," OTP, p. 158)

When one compares the Moabite version of the war with the account in 2 Kgs 3, it becomes evident that preserving the facts of the battle was not the primary concern of the biblical writers. Instead the narrators focus on the difference between "good kings" and "bad kings." The narrators evaluate monarchs by comparing them with Jeroboam. If they had "walked in the way of Jeroboam" (1 Kgs 15:34; 16:19), they were considered evil kings who brought destruction to the land and deserved no aid from God or the prophets. By contrast, God's covenant promise obligated God to come to the aid of righteous kings.

One additional theme in the cycle of stories about Elisha is **universalism.** This theme is often associated with the assertion of Yahweh's power. In 2 Kgs 5, a Syrian general makes this declaration of Yahweh's universal power. Naaman is a high-ranking military commander who has been afflicted with leprosy. When all other cures fail, Naaman takes the advice of his wife's Israelite slave girl and consults Elisha. He must engage in some difficult political maneuvering to gain safe passage into Israel, which is considered enemy territory, but eventually he comes to Elisha's house (5:5–9). He never gets to see the prophet face-to-face. Instead Elisha's servant Gehazi relays instructions to the general. This is neither proper etiquette nor an impressive demonstration of prophetic power. Sensing that he has been snubbed, Naaman nearly storms off in anger. His servants, however, convince him to attempt the cure suggested by the prophet, and so he dips himself seven times in the Jordan River.

Universalism

In their portrayal of Yahweh as supreme among the gods, the biblical writers periodically inject the theme of universalism into the narratives. In such narratives, a non-Israelite character makes a statement of faith that Yahweh is the most powerful or the only true god. The character makes this declaration because she has come to know what Yahweh has done for the Israelites, as in the case of Rahab (Josh 2:9–10), or because he has had a personal experience of Yahweh's power. Although the theme of Yahweh's universally manifest power eventually develops into the concept of monotheism, or an exclusive belief that Yahweh is the only God, this concept will not be fully fleshed out until late in Israelite history, perhaps not until after 400 B.C.E.

Cured of his leprosy, Naaman rushes back to reward Elisha. In his enthusiasm, he declares, "Now I know there is no God in all the earth except in Israel" (5:15). The narrative thus develops the theme of universalism described above. Although the thankful general presses Elisha to accept a gift for his services, the prophet refuses any payment. It is possible that Elisha's refusal is based on his attempt to differentiate himself from priests or professional healers or miracle workers, who performed their cures for a fee. The prophet, however, clearly wants it understood that the healing came from Yahweh and was a demonstration of God's power, extended even to persons outside the covenant.

The general then asks Elisha for a future consideration. As part of his role as adviser to the Syrian king, Naaman was expected to participate in an annual religious ritual honoring their god Rimmon. He assures the prophet this will in no way conflict with his new devotion to Yahweh, and he proves this by requesting two loads of Israelite soil to take back with him to Syria (5:17). His request for Israelite soil reflects the belief that gods are localized within the lands in which they are worshiped. By taking soil back to Syria, Naaman believes he is physically extending the presence of Yahweh into his own country.

Elisha's end is as mysterious as that of his master, Elijah, and this is reflected in the mysterious power associated with his tomb. Apparently, the site of Elisha's burial was forgotten. Later the tomb was reopened and a corpse was lowered into place. When a band of raiders interrupted the burial party, they simply abandoned the body in their escape. When the dead man's body fell among Elisha's bones, the corpse revived, jumped from the tomb, and ran after his friends (13:20–21). Just as Elijah's mantle had functioned as an object of power, so too did Elisha's bones. In the future, however, it will be the words, not the relics, of the prophets that will demonstrate the power of God.

6

THE BOOK OF AMOS

At the time that Amos was called to be a prophet, he was living in a small village called Tekoa in the Judean highlands. It is hard to imagine a more out-of-the-way or unlikely place for a prophet to come from. World events must have seemed very far away from Tekoa, a village of perhaps 150 people, and yet these events will conspire to draw him into the public arena. Amos's mission will be to travel north to the kingdom of Israel, a country that was ruled at the time by Jeroboam II (786–746 B.C.E.). Both Israel and Judah were enjoying a period of peace and prosperity. This was the result of the capture of Damascus, the capital of Syria, by the Assyrian king Shalmaneser III in 802 B.C.E. The elimination of Israel's chief economic and military rival gave the rulers of the northern kingdom more latitude in making **treaties** and in dealing with neighboring countries. Israelite merchants also enjoyed this period of freedom to trade in previously restricted areas and thus were able to increase their fortunes. Of course, this is only a respite before the Assyrians once again begin to expand their **hegemony** into all of Syria-Palestine. By the end of the eighth century, an exhausted Israel will be conquered, its capital city destroyed, and much of its populace deported. Amos's task will be to warn the Israelites of this coming disaster and to show them how to prevent their own cultural extinction before it is too late.

Amos is the first of the eighth-century prophets and the first of the so-called classical prophets, whose messages appear in books bearing their names. Since he is a farmer living in the small Judean village ten miles south of Jerusalem, his world has been a relatively small one. He is skilled in a variety of tasks associated with life on a small farm (Amos 7:14), but he is not a Levite and does not appear to have had any formal education beyond what would have been available in the village. Despite this, God calls him to serve as a prophet and, more important, a prophet to the people of the northern kingdom of Israel. Amos's social and physical location will set the tone for his message and attitude.

Amos is a very angry prophet. He condemns the people of Israel for their social injustices and their unorthodox worship practices. The prophet appears relieved that he can deliver his message and then return home. In this sense, he is emotionally disconnected from his audience and may therefore feel freer to condemn them. He shows very little compassion and offers only a very strict adherence to the **covenant** as a guide to deliverance. He does speak of the possibility of redemption in his calls to "seek **Yahweh** and live" (5:6, 14–15), but he only hints at the possibility that the Lord "may . . . be gracious to the remnant of Joseph" (5:15). To further reinforce his message, the prophet warns Israel against having any confidence in its shrines or the monarchy (see 4:4; 6:8; compare Jer 7:15).

The memories of the division of the kingdom at the end of the ninth century and of king Jeroboam's sins serve as a backdrop to Amos's message (see 1 Kgs 12:25–33). Recognizing that his people still looked to Jerusalem as the religious center where sacrifices were to be made, Jeroboam had initiated a series of religious reforms. Although these reforms made good political sense, they became the basis for subsequent criticism of Israel and the kings who continued to promote the **"sins of Jeroboam."**

The Sins of Jeroboam

Rival shrines are dedicated at Dan and Bethel.

Golden calves are placed in the shrines as substitutes for the **ark of the covenant.**

High places *(bamôt)* are tolerated in local village culture.

Non-Levites are appointed to serve as priests.

A revised religious calendar is mandated for the major festivals.

The harshness of Amos's message suggests that he does not really believe that Israel and its people will repent and thus survive the coming destruction. He even refers to the nation as a "remnant" before foreign invaders (Amos 5:15) have culled it. Given this gloomy future, Amos does not waste words on deaf ears. He simply tells them all what they need to know to live and leaves it to them to act on this advice.

Amos wisely begins his message with a rhetorical strategy that will draw a crowd (1:3–2:8). Starting with Damascus (Syria) in the northeast and then turning south to Gaza in Philistia, Amos condemns Israel's political rivals. He then denounces Israel's economic partners and neighboring states: Tyre (Phoenicia), Edom, Ammon, Moab, and even Judah. In each case, he begins his denunciation with the formula "For three transgressions of _____, and for four, I will not revoke the punishment." He then recites the transgressions of each kingdom and announces God's punishment. One can easily imagine that the growing crowd would have cheered and urged Amos to continue—at least until he reached his intended goal, the condemnation of Israel itself. It is not recorded whether they melted away when Amos began his list of charges against Israel, but after what they had heard, they surely knew what the prophet had in store for them.

SOCIAL INJUSTICE

Amos's critique of Israel begins at 2:6 and centers on violations of the **egalitarian** ideal that is so often championed by the prophets (see above). Amos condemns social injustices and challenges those "who trample the head of the poor into the dust of the earth" (2:7). He uses concrete imagery to capture the horror of these crimes. He condemns the practice of bribing judges as "selling the righteous for silver" (2:6a). Other probably legal strategies for dealing with the repayment of debt also provoke Amos's ire. For example, he ridicules the practice of selling persons into debt slavery for defaulting on very small loans as "[selling] the needy for a pair of sandals" (2:6b). And using "garments taken in pledge" (2:8a) is tantamount to stealing from the poor. Finally, Amos condemns the unjust business practices of using false balances ("make the ephah small and the shekel great," 8:5b) and selling bags of contaminated grain (8:6b).

It is likely that Amos is drawing on well-known **wisdom** traditions as well as on real-life situations. Another peasant farmer, this one from Middle Kingdom Egypt (2134–1786 B.C.E.), spoke of the responsibility of the wealthy and the powerful to provide justice and fair treatment to the poor and the weak:

> You are the chief steward, you are my lord. . . . You father the orphan, you husband the widow. . . . [But t]hose who distribute the grain put more in their own ration. Those authorized to give full measures short their people. Lawmakers approve of robbery. ("A Farmer and the Courts in Egypt," *OTP*, pp. 217, 219)

Amos knew that justice was not always readily available to day laborers or bond servants, who owned no land, did not operate businesses, and had only the clothes on their backs to serve as a guarantee that they would do a full day's work. One such man in the late seventh century B.C.E. had a scribe write a letter to the governor pleading for his rights and dignity in much the same way that Amos championed the debt slaves:

> Your servant was harvesting. . . . The work went as usual and your servant completed the harvesting and hauling which I was assigned. . . . Despite the fact . . . Hoshaiahu came and took your servant's garment . . . Please intercede for me so that my garment will be returned and I will, as always, do my share of the work. ("Yavne Yam Letter," *OTP*, pp. 329–30)

Both this letter and Amos's **oracle** call on the authorities to adhere to the legal principle found in Exod 22:26–27. The poor were not to be so abused that they were left to shiver through the night without their cloaks. They might have only this garment to serve as collateral and surety that they would work an honest day's labor, but they were to be treated with respect and not reduced to the indignity of naked slaves.

Amos holds back none of his indignation as he describes the indifferent stance of the wealthy toward the poor. **Archaeological** evidence from eighth-century B.C.E. settlements in Israel and Judah suggests that the monarchy and its supporters exercised increasing control over the economy. Royal herds were increased (2 Chr 26:10), and large tracts of land were systematically enclosed and farmed to produce ever greater quantities of grain, olive oil, and wine. Although these efforts supported increased trade and the influx of luxury and manufactured goods, many of the small land-owners were driven off their property and into the employ of the state or the uncertain life of day laborers. Thus Amos is justified in describing the wives of the greedy merchants and leaders of Samaria as sleek "cows of Bashan," who fatten themselves indul-gently on other people's grain and call for more. When the city of Samaria falls, they will be dragged through the breaches in the walls, and their impaled bodies will be flung into a dung heap (Amos 4:1–3). Their fine houses, decorated with ivory, will be torn down and abandoned (3:15).

HYPOCRISY

Amos also addresses the theme of religious hypocrisy. He asserts that the people's worship is useless because it is conducted without true faith (2:7). The prophet also reflects on the greedy merchants who cannot even wait for the **Sabbath** or other reli-gious holidays to end so that they can resume business (8:5a). Their greed obviously far outweighs their piety.

It is not surprising that the prophet is so bitter. He cannot understand how the people can fail to recognize that it is God who gives them their wealth. It amazes him that they do not understand the signs of God's displeasure. Disasters such as famine ("cleanness of teeth") selective droughts ("one field would be rained upon" and another left to wither; compare Hag 1:10–11), "blight and mil-dew," and locusts and pestilence (Amos 4:6–10) were all intended to bring the people back to God. They celebrate festivals and call solemn assemblies, but they do not create the just society that God desires for his people:

> I hate, I despise your festivals, and I take no delight in your solemn assemblies. Even though you offer me your burnt offerings and grain offerings, I will not accept them. . . . But let justice roll down like waters, and righteousness like an ever-flowing stream. (5:21–24)

Like Samuel, Amos declares that "it is better to obey than sacrifice" (1 Sam 15:22). Isaiah and Jeremiah will follow Amos when they condemn the hollow worship of their people:

> Bringing offerings is futile; incense is an abomination to me. New moon and sabbath and calling of convocation—I cannot endure solemn assemblies with iniquity. (Isa 1:13)

> Of what use to me is frankincense that comes from Sheba, or sweet cane from a distant land? Your burnt offerings are not acceptable, nor are your sacrifices pleasing to me. (Jer 6:20)

Amos focuses his venom on the rival temple at Bethel, which was established as a high place by Jeroboam I when the kingdom was divided. He sarcastically "encourages" the people to come to Bethel to make their offerings and tithes there and to have the amounts of their offerings published for all to hear (Amos 4:4–5). Then he tells them that Yahweh has completely rejected Israel's worship as unacceptable and as so much "noise" (5:21–24).

Eventually the authorities can stand no more of this confrontational prophet. Amaziah, the high priest of Bethel, writes to king Jeroboam II and also publicly charges Amos with making both treasonous and blasphemous statements. He ridicules Amos and sarcastically calls him a "seer," a term that implies special abilities and perhaps may be applied to diviners (compare 1 Sam 9:9). It is possible that Amaziah is exercising his powers to control speech within the sacred precincts of the temple at Bethel. The Jerusalem priest Zephaniah will have a similar charge during Jeremiah's day; his responsibility will be to "control any madman who plays the prophet" (Jer 29:26). Amos rejects the priest's charge that he has no right to speak in the "king's sanctuary" (Amos 7:10–12), and he stands on his rights as one who has been called to perform this service for Yahweh. Amos's account of his call is quite simple but adequate to meet Amaziah's charges: "the LORD took me from following the flock, and the LORD said to me, 'Go, prophesy to my people Israel'" (7:15). While his account does not compare in style to the very elaborate call stories found in Isaiah and Jeremiah, it contains just as much power, since it describes the way that God has intruded into his life. Like Isaiah and Jeremiah, Amos did not ask for the job. In all three cases, God thrusts it upon them.

Unlike Amaziah, who owes his position to the king's patronage, Amos has no "establishment" credentials. Amos tells Amaziah, "I am no prophet, nor a prophet's son" (7:14). In this way he reasserts the position that prophets are free agents working directly for Yahweh and not requiring any certification other than the truth of their message. He also justifies his mission to Bethel, a place that signifies Israel's disobedience to the covenant.

Although Amos leaves little hope for the nation of Israel in his statements, there is a brief use of the **remnant** theme in Amos 5. Here he simply tells the people to "seek God and live" (5:4, 6) so that Yahweh will have an excuse to relent and lessen their punishment. But unlike similar passages, where the people fully expect God to have mercy (see Jer 26:19), Amos's statement seems to offer only a brief glimmer of hope. This is all he will hold out to them. The only break in this generally gloomy picture is found in Amos 9:11–15, which describes the restoration of the Davidic kingdom and a return of the land's prosperity. Since this glimpse of a brighter future is more appropriate to the message of the prophets of the late monarchy (Jer 30:18–22; Ezek 39:21–29) and the exile (Isa 43:19–21), it is probably a later addition to the book of Amos.

Amos warns the people not to look forward to the "Day of Yahweh" (Amos 5:18–20), for it will bring them judgment, not greater prosperity. This very earthy prophet draws on his life experiences as a farmer and herdsman and uses the pastoral images of his country background. He describes the people of Israel as "summer fruit" (8:2)—sweet and full of initial promise but quick to decay and to become worthless. Such an image surely must have struck an ominous chord with some of them as the Assyrian specter of power moved inexorably westward into Syria-Palestine.

7

THE BOOK OF HOSEA

Unlike his eighth-century contemporary Amos, the prophet Hosea speaks to his own people. Although his message is harsh, he offers more hope that reconciliation with **Yahweh** is still possible. Hosea speaks at the end of an era. The reign of Jeroboam II is about to come to an end, and his successors are weaklings, fighting among themselves. Under the leadership of Tiglath-pileser III (744–727 B.C.E.), Assyria now emerges as a real international force. Israel comes under the control of Assyria first as a client state, then as a bound vassal. Assyria finally destroys Israel in 721 B.C.E. because of its repeated revolts against Assyrian domination. In this desperate period, Hosea almost ignores the Assyrian threat and instead concentrates on what he perceives as the root causes of Israel's problems—idolatry and a squandering of the land's **covenantal** potential.

IDOLATRY

The first three chapters of Hosea present the prophet's principal themes in a tightly woven, **enacted prophecy** involving his marriage to a woman named Gomer, who proves to be unfaithful. The chapters pose two intriguing questions. First, was Hosea a Levite? If so, then in the northern kingdom he would have been unable to function as a priest, since the **sins of Jeroboam** would have excluded him from the cult. Second, was Gomer a prostitute before Hosea married her? If so, then the tension between his prophetic role and his priestly background would be heightened, since a Levite would have been forbidden by law to marry a prostitute (see Lev 21:14–15).

There is no consensus among scholars on either issue. Certainly, it is not necessary for Hosea to have been a Levite for the metaphor to work. What matters is that Hosea's dysfunctional marriage serves as a metaphor for Yahweh's difficult relationship with Israel. In the terms of this metaphor, Gomer's promiscuity symbolizes Israel's blatant idolatry. Hosea, in turn, represents in fact and in metaphor the long-suffering husband/God, who laments his wife's/Israel's actions and determines to dissolve the covenant between them.

Hosea's marriage to Gomer produces three children, each of whom is given a symbolic name, a form of enacted prophecy.

Jezreel is named for the strategic valley where Jehu defeated Ahab's son, took the throne of Israel, and established his own dynasty (2 Kgs 9:15–26). The name implies that the reigning king, a descendant of Jehu, owes his power to Yahweh's intervention. Since this is the case, his power can just as easily be taken away. The Jezreel Valley is the most fertile area of Israel; thus Yahweh's threats to "take back my grain . . . and my wine in its season" (Hos 2:9) suggest both famine and the potential for political unrest. The child's name sounds a warning that the covenant relationship is about to be dissolved.

The name of the second child, Not Pitied *(Lo-ruhamah)*, condemns the social injustice of Hosea's time. The prophet angrily indicts those who worsen the plight of the poor and the weak. The name suggests that Yahweh will not pity Israel when its punishment comes.

The name of the third child, Not My People *(Lo-ammi)*, revokes Israel's identity as the people of Yahweh. It is hard to imagine a more terrible rejection of Israel. This people had prided itself as God's chosen nation. The covenant had assured the Israelites that Yahweh would provide them with land and children (compare 2:8–9). Because they had been unfaithful to Yahweh and had ascribed their abundant harvests to Baal, they had destroyed the covenant (2:13). The name also has a second meaning, since it suggests that Hosea suspected the child was not actually his.

Given the evidence of Gomer's unfaithfulness, Hosea has no choice but to confront her. One can compare Hosea's actions with the legal injunction in Num 5:31, which deals with cases of suspected adultery. A husband who has been incensed by a "spirit of jealousy" because he suspects that his wife has been unfaithful must bring her before a priest for a trial by ordeal. While Hosea does not employ this legal strategy, he does ask the children to reason with her to get her to abandon her infidelities (Hos 2:2).

When reason fails, Hosea severely punishes Gomer. He secludes her (2:6), strips her of her finery (2:3; compare Ezek 16:37–39), drives her from his home, and divorces her (Hos 2:9–12; compare Mal 2:15–16). The divorce is symbolized by his withdrawing grain, wine, and other products that were her due as a wife in good standing (compare Exod 21:10). Just as these actions signal the end of Hosea's marriage, they also indicate the end of Israel's covenant with Yahweh.

> **Benefits of the Covenant Agreement**
>
> If you heed these ordinances, by diligently observing them, the LORD your God will maintain with you the covenant loyalty that he swore to your ancestors; he will love you, bless you, and multiply you; he will bless the fruit of your womb and fruit of your ground, your grain and your wine and your oil, the increase of your cattle and the issue of your flock, in the land that he swore to your ancestors to give you. (Deut 7:12–13)

It should be noted that the elements of the marriage metaphor could lead to a dangerous reading of the text. Hosea's treatment of his wife and his children (Hos 2:4–5) has sometimes been used to justify similar actions in modern relationships as well. This is a perversion of the biblical narrative and of the intent of the passage. Hosea 1–3 is not a story about the absolute submission of wives to their husbands, nor does it give license to husbands to brutalize their wives for real or imagined transgressions. The symbolism here refers to the actions that God intends to take against the unfaithful nation of Israel—famine, exile, and slavery.

Yahweh seeks to restore the nation and to forgive Israel, and this is again reflected in the metaphor of Hosea's marriage. Hosea agrees to take Gomer back if she renounces her other lovers forever and acknowledges that only he is her lord (2:14–20). Hosea's actions mirror Yahweh's, who will take Israel back if she renounces her Baals. When Gomer returns, Hosea acknowledges that their children, whom he rejected as "children of whoredom," are in fact his heirs (see CH 170–171). The children's symbolic names are now reversed as fertility returns to the land and God establishes a new covenant with Israel (Hos 2:21–23).

> If a citizen, who has children by his wife and by his slave, adopts the slave's children, then his household shall be divided evenly between the children of both, after his wife's first-born son receives the preferential share. ("Code of Hammurabi 170," *OTP*, p. 106)

Hosea's allusion to the Valley of Achor (Hos 2:15) underscores what is at stake in Yahweh's offer of reconciliation. This was the place where Achan and his family had been stoned to death for his violation of the *herem* (holy war) during the battle of Jericho. By stealing from the loot captured at Jericho, Achan had defiled all of the Israelites, not just himself (Josh 7:22–26). Consequently, the fate of the entire nation was at stake, and the conquest could not continue until Achan acknowledged his guilt and accepted his punishment. The allusion to Achor in relation to Gomer's sin indicates that God could restore the covenant only if Israel truly became faithful to Yahweh once again.

Hosea associates Israel's worship of the Baals with their misuse of the land. Some of the powerful and wealthy individuals took advantage of a weakening economy to amass land, either by cheating their neighbors out of their land or by using the courts to their own advantage (compare 1 Kgs 21). Since the covenant promised land to each Israelite household, Hosea regards this misuse as a clear violation of the covenant. He accuses them of becoming so corrupt that they "remove the landmark," the sacred boundary stones that marked off land ownership (Hos 5:10). Hosea assures them that these actions will draw down upon the nation the full force of God's wrath (compare Isa 5:8).

Boundary Markers

Do not topple the markers on the boundaries of a field, or your conscience will destroy you. To please the pharaoh, our divine ruler, observe the borders of your neighbors' fields. ("Teachings of Amen-em-ope," *OTP*, p. 277)

Do not remove the ancient landmark that your ancestors set up. (Prov 22:28)

Do not remove an ancient landmark or encroach on the fields of orphans. (Prov 23:10)

KNOWLEDGE OF GOD

A second theme developed in the book of Hosea is that of the "knowledge of God." Hosea condemns two leadership groups, the monarchy and the priesthood, for failing to provide the people with the knowledge they need to obey the covenant (Hos 4:1–6; 5:1). The rampant idolatry and **syncretistic cultic** practices of Israel's shrines and priesthood are chronicled in Hosea's repeated condemnations: "With their silver and gold they made idols for their own destruction" (8:4b). They consciously make sacrifices to Yahweh as well as other gods. This is quite understandable in the context of the polytheism of their neighbors, who wished to placate and obtain the favor of as many deities as possible. Such offerings will be rejected by Yahweh, however, who demands their exclusive worship: "Though they offer choice sacrifices, though they eat flesh, the LORD does not accept them" (8:13).

The Israelites' efforts are unacceptable because they do not understand what is truly expected of them: "For I desire steadfast love and not sacrifice, the knowledge of God rather than burnt offerings" (6:6). The term that Hosea uses to parallel knowledge in this passage is "steadfast love." The Hebrew word is *hesed*, which is variously translated as "love," "abiding love," "steadfast love," "everlasting love," and "mercy." This is a technical legal term found most often in **treaty** language and especially in passages in which the covenant is spelled out for the people.

Hesed in Covenantal Context

Hesed is used in the context of a request by Abraham's servant that God adhere to a treaty obligation to make Abraham the father of many nations (Gen 24:12, 14, 27).

Hesed appears in the Ten Commandments as part of Yahweh's commitment to the covenant promise (Exod 20:6).

Hesed is used to reinforce the solemnity of a slave's contractual declaration of perpetual servitude: "I love my master, my wife, and my children" (Exod 21:5).

Hesed is an expression of faithfulness on the part of those who would keep the covenant: "who love me and keep my commandments" (Deut 5:10).

Hesed functions as part of the **covenant renewal ceremony** staged by Joshua to celebrate the conquest of the land and to renew the Israelites' commitment to serve Yahweh: "to love the LORD your God, to walk in his way, to keep his commandments" (Josh 22:5).

Hesed is the term God uses to reassure the people of divine compliance with the terms of the covenant: "I act with steadfast love, justice, and righteousness" (Jer 9:24).

Hosea's use of treaty language is reminiscent of Samuel's condemnation of Saul for failing to keep God's commandments (1 Sam 15:22). The difference, however, is that the people lack the knowledge they need to be able to obey (Hos 4:6). Their destruction has become inevitable because their leaders have failed to instruct them in the terms of the covenant: "a people without understanding comes to ruin" (4:14). Like Gomer, who has been a bad example and a poor teacher for her children, the kings and priests of Israel teach only accommodation with foreign cultures, not a strict adherence to Yahweh worship (5:1–4).

Hosea is certain that Assyria will defeat Israel's kings and take away their idols and temple treasures as spoil (10:3–8). Still, Hosea cannot leave his own people to be destroyed without warning them of the coming destruction. This is coupled with an assurance that, though Yahweh will punish them, the punishment will be that of a parent correcting a wayward child (11:1–7). This parenting theme is one that strikes true to every parent who knows the frustrations of guiding a child through to adulthood:

> The more I called them, the more they went from me. . . . Yet it was I who taught Ephraim to walk, I took them up in my arms; but they did not know that I healed them. (11:3–4)

Yahweh cries out, "How can I give you up, Ephraim?" (11:8) while acknowledging that Israel's return to the land will come only after they have been punished for their deceitful behavior (12:2). Once they have discovered that "Assyria shall not save us" (14:3), Yahweh may redeem them. Before this can happen, however, they must return in faithfulness to Yahweh (14:4–7), just as Gomer had to be faithful to Hosea. They and their land can be healed and restored, but first they must regain their lost knowledge of Yahweh's power and the covenant.

8

THE BOOK OF ISAIAH

Isaiah is the longest and structurally the most complex of
the prophetic books in the Hebrew Bible. Its chapters reflect at
least three separate time periods: ca. 739–687 B.C.E.; 540–535
B.C.E.; and 515–500 B.C.E. The traditionally accepted sections of
the book, Isa 1–39, 40–55, and 56–66, correspond to these time
periods. The prophet Isaiah is mentioned by name only sixteen
times throughout the entire book; this suggests a deliberate
effort to depersonalize the text, giving the message of **Yahweh**
more prominence than the prophet who delivers it. This is the
case in the latter two segments of the book, which were written
well past the time of the original Isaiah and thus do not depend
upon his public pronouncements. Each section of the book will
be dealt with in chronological order at appropriate places in this
volume.

In this segment we will discuss the first Isaiah, or Isaiah of
Jerusalem, who dates to the period of the late eighth and early
seventh centuries B.C.E. Unlike either of his contemporaries, Amos
or Hosea, he seems to have free access to the king. He speaks
authoritatively, and there appears to have been no official opposition to his very harsh **oracles.** Although the text is not explicit on
this point, he may well have been a member of the religious

establishment in the temple in Jerusalem. Isaiah's message is that of a well-educated man committed to the Davidic monarchy, to the temple, and to Jerusalem/Zion as the place where God has caused his name to dwell. Even so, as a prophet he condemns individual Davidic kings, the temple community, and the inhabitants of Judah and Jerusalem for their failure to keep the **covenant** with Yahweh. They will have to face the consequences of their covenant violations. By the end of Isaiah's career, the land of Judah will be devastated.

ISAIAH'S CALL

The story of Isaiah's **call** does not appear until Isa 6, a fact that seems strange to modern readers, who quite naturally would expect that a book about Isaiah's message would begin with his call to become a prophet. Whatever the reason for placing the story at this point in the book, the account of Isaiah's call is as familiar to modern Western readers as any part of the Old Testament because Handel used it as the opening text for his *Messiah*. The elements of the call help us to date it, since Isaiah tells us that it happened in the year King Uzziah died, about 739 B.C.E. The mention of seraphim in 6:2 is likely based on the design of the **ark of the covenant,** which had crossed wings on the lid representing angels upholding the throne of God (Exod 25:17–22; see also 1 Kgs 6:23–28). Because of this imagery, it is possible that Isaiah had this vision while he was in the temple in Jerusalem.

In Isaiah's vision, the various manifestations of power all exhibit Yahweh's control over creation. An earthquake shakes the pivots of the doors, symbolizing the presence of a force no door can shut out or in. A cloaking smoke then fills the temple and adds elements of tension and mystery, which are also found in previous **theophanies** (see Exod 19:16–18). Also familiar from Moses' theophanic experience is Isaiah's demurral. When he is confronted with the challenge of prophetic service, Isaiah protests that his lips are mortal and therefore "unclean," or ritually impure, and thus he cannot speak the holy words of Yahweh. If Isaiah was a priest, he would have been particularly concerned about matters of **ritual purity** and conscious of the great distance between the mortal and divine realms.

Simply stating the obvious, however, does not serve as an acceptable excuse to decline God's call. A quick remedy comes in this vision as an angel takes a burning coal from the altar fire and spiritually cauterizes Isaiah's lips with a holy fire. This cleansing empowers him to speak the words God gives him to speak (Isa 6:6–7). Once his impediment has been removed, he hears the voice of God asking, "who will go for me?" Isaiah can only respond, "Here am I! Send me" (6:8; compare 1 Sam 3:1–14).

Isaiah's commission is not an easy one. In the face of the mounting threat of Assyrian invasion, Isaiah is to speak, but the people will neither hear nor understand. The nation has rejected all previous warnings, and now Yahweh intends to allow Assyria to destroy their cities and take their people into exile (compare Amos 5:10–13). Despite this inevitable punishment, a **remnant** will survive and serve as a "holy seed" to restore the nation (Isa 6:13).

One aspect of the story of Isaiah's call that should be emphasized is its use of the term "holy." Isaiah employs it as the opposite of "human." But human behavior could become holy, just as Isaiah's lips have been empowered to speak holy words. The people in turn could model themselves after the "Holy One of Israel," whose covenant and laws provide the direction for ethical behavior. In this prophet's message, the familiar themes of social justice, the obligation to aid and not oppress the weak, and the obligation to worship only Yahweh become the keys to holiness. This, of course, is not unique to Isaiah. Injunctions against profaning Yahweh's holy name are found throughout the prophets (Jer 34:16; Amos 2:7; Ezek 36:22–32).

ORACLES OF WARNING

Two examples of Isaiah's message will be presented here to illustrate the manner in which he announces judgment and offers the people a choice. The first is found in Isa 1:10–23, where the prophet plays upon the familiar tradition of the destruction of Sodom and Gomorrah (Gen 19) as well as the past experience of Israel regarding Yahweh's interaction with his people. Like Amos, Isaiah condemns worship as nothing but empty rituals (compare Amos 5:21–24). Yahweh refuses to listen to hollow prayers or to accept meaningless offerings. Instead he calls for social justice— what the covenant had stipulated as the basic requirement for life with God. Yahweh thus gives the people a choice. If they are willing to cleanse themselves of the innocent blood that they have shed in oppressing the weak (Isa 1:16–17), then redemption is possible. If they do not choose the way of righteousness, however, war and destruction are implicitly threatened, "for the mouth of the LORD has spoken" (1:20).

In his "Song of the Vineyard" (5:1–7), Isaiah indicts both the kings and the people of Judah. The setting for the song is the gathering of celebrants at the time of the harvest festival. The grape harvest is such a fundamental experience of the land's fertility that it became a familiar metaphor of prosperity and divine blessing in the biblical tradition (2 Kgs 18:31; Zech 3:10). Isaiah takes full advantage of the people's joy and expectation as they labor at the winepress. But as is typical of many prophets, he turns what should have been a song of joy into a cry against injustice. In painstaking detail, the prophet sketches out Yahweh's case against the people.

This song depicts Yahweh as an owner who lavishly tends his vineyard and quite naturally expects his labors to bear fruit. It is useful to read this song as a contrast to Deuteronomy's depiction of the bounty of the promised land. There the people are said to inherit a region that has already been tamed by previous inhabitants, who have already hewn cisterns from the soft limestone hillsides and whose vineyards and olive groves are well established (Deut 6:11). The Israelites do not even have to work to get the water for their crops as they did in Egypt, where farming depended on labor-intensive irrigation. Instead seasonal rains loosen the ground for planting and encourage growth (Deut 11:10–12).

By contrast, the song in Isaiah more realistically describes the arduous process of preparing and working a hillside vineyard in the Judean countryside. Hard and heavy labor was a necessity. The first step was the construction of terraces, which were designed to minimize erosion and to provide sufficient farming space to meet the needs of small villages. Terracing also ensured that the vines received the requisite amount of moisture during the critical winter months, when the leaves appear and the shoots and root system begin to grow. Like other crops, grapevines can be damaged by too little water, by over irrigation, or by watering too late in the season.

By the time of Isaiah, terraces were being installed on slopes that had been harvested of their lumber and badly eroded. To counteract the damage, farmers built retaining walls and brought in new topsoil from elsewhere to fill the terraces. Isaiah 5:1–7 probably describes the reconstruction of such a terrace as Yahweh digs the soil, clears the stones, and plants the vines. When Isaiah describes the vineyard as lying on "a very fertile hill" (5:1), it is because backbreaking labor has made it so.

Once the land has been prepared, the vines are planted. This act serves in the prophetic literature as a sign of Yahweh's establishment of the covenant with Israel. Just having the opportunity to develop such a vineyard is described by Jeremiah (Jer 35:7) as the sign of sedentary existence as compared with the nomadic life of the landless who do not share in the covenant. Drawing on this covenantal metaphor of planting a vineyard, Ezek 17:5–6 describes the setting of seedlings in fertile and well-watered ground, where roots could find strong purchase and leaves and vines could stretch across the ground luxuriantly.

Planting the cuttings is only the first step. The farmer must keep the vineyard free of moisture-sapping weeds, briars, and thorns. In some cases, the farmer could use a plow to keep the weeds under control, but narrow areas would have to be hoed regularly by hand (Isa 7:25) during the growing season. Then, during the first six years of growth (Lev 25:3), the farmer would prune the maturing vines (Isa 2:4) in the winter months to remove a portion of the previous season's growth (4 Macc 1:29). This pruning would enhance the growth of the remaining grape clusters (2 Esd 16:43). Additional pruning in the early summer months (May and June according to the Gezer Calendar) would remove unproductive tendrils and dead vegetation (Isa 18:5; John 15:2).

The wise farmer also took measures to protect his vines and their fruit from foraging by small animals (Song 2:15) and travelers (Prov 24:30–31). Accordingly, the owner of the vineyard in Isa 5 constructs both a hedge and a stone wall to guard the vineyard from harm. He also builds a watchtower to shelter the laborers and to serve as a lookout for marauding bands of animals or humans. Probably not every farmer could afford to go to such lengths to protect his fields, but in Isaiah's song, in which Yahweh is the owner, all of the various means of protection are chronicled. Thus the image is one of a divine owner who makes every effort to create a fertile field, lays out the choicest cuttings, and then provides protection from all dangers from without.

Isaiah's song also mentions the installation of a wine vat, which would have been carved out of the soft limestone of the hillside. Like the threshing floor, the wine vat was a communal operation (see Hos 9:2). Not every farmer would need his own, but every laborer would be engaged in treading grapes at harvest time. As one team of workers exhausted itself, another would take its place until all of the ripe grapes that had been set aside for wine production had been crushed to pulp. The workers kept themselves energized and in rhythm by singing or chanting (Isa 16:10), accompanied by music performed by their wives and daughters (Judg 21:20–21), and perhaps with the anticipation of the fruits of their labor. Egyptian depictions of the treaders show that their efforts are synchronized to the beat of batons or clappers.

The harvesting of the grapes from mature vines would take place in late summer, when new growth has stopped and the bark darkens (Num 13:20). At this point, the grapes were tasted to determine when they were ready to be taken to the winepress. This would be the stage at which the owner or his overseer could judge the quality of the grapes (Isa 5:2c). If the grapes were sour, such as those mentioned in Ezekiel's proverb (Ezek 18:2), they may have been picked too early and thus have not yet produced enough sugar to make them sweet.

But the grapes in Yahweh's vineyard are sour for another reason. Isaiah says that the vineyard produced "wild grapes," not unripe ones. Jeremiah also uses this metaphor of a "reliable" stock of grapes that inexplicably were transformed into a "putrid" or "foreign" variety (Jer 2:21). Jeremiah's play on words points to influences beyond the normal control of the vintner. Clearly the vine is at fault. So also in Isaiah: this vine is acting unnaturally. Its normal cycle has been interrupted, and its fruit never adequately ripens. What remains is worthless, lacking in any nourishing value, and totally unfit for its intended use. The labor that went into the construction of the terraced vineyard and its cultivation can yield nothing if the vines have gone bad. All that can be expected, given these conditions, is an empty field where "no songs are sung, no shouts are raised; no treader treads out wine in the presses" (Isa 16:10). Yahweh concludes, "What more was there to do for my vineyard that I have not done in it?" (5:4a).

Such evil cannot be borne, for the land is precious and the time expended by the owner and the laborers cannot be recovered. And so, Isaiah's song concludes with a very harsh punishment. God renounces all interest or concern in any future dealings with this vineyard. Its terraces, walls, soil, and vines are to be thrown down and left in a state that can only be compared to the condition of cities that have been abandoned by their gods (see the Sumerian poems on the "Laments for Ur"). With the terraces destroyed, the soil will erode away and what remains will nurture only thorns and weeds. Wild animals will prowl through this once-civilized place. The final insult is that Yahweh will withhold the rains. This spells disaster for all and is generally taken in ancient Near Eastern literature to be a sign of divine displeasure.

> When the storm subsides, the city is in ruins. . . . The dead are scattered everywhere. . . . The walls are breached, the main gates are blocked with corpses. . . . The main streets are choked with dead. . . . Where crowds once celebrated festivals bodies lay in every street, corpses piled on every road. ("Laments for Ur," *OTP*, p. 236)

At the end of the song, Israel and Judah are identified as the vine (Isa 5:7). What has made Yahweh's "vines" go bad are unjust practices and the shedding of innocent blood. These injustices include depriving the poor of their lands by creating huge estates (5:8), drunkenness and self-indulgent living (5:11–12), public deception by the leaders (5:18–21), and bribery (5:23). The result is to be a ruined land, just as the vineyard was laid waste. The nation will be left open to the assaults of other people (5:26–30), and the "chosen" who "are wise in [their] own eyes" will go into exile because of their lack of knowledge (5:13; compare Hos 4:1, 2).

It may be that Isaiah understood this destruction as preparation for a new beginning (see Isa 1:24–28). Massive destructive events, such as floods and earthquakes, were often understood as preparation for the creation of a new, cleansed world. If this is the case, then, the complete destruction of the vineyard signals the end of the old world of the monarchy and unfaithfulness to the covenant. Once every trace of the old and corrupt world is removed, the stage is set for a new beginning. In this new creation, the new "vines" will escape the fate of the first vineyard because they will have been cleansed of the internal corruption that led to destruction in the first place.

Now that we have examined Isaiah's "Song of the Vineyard," we find that it is also appropriate to think of it as a juridical parable. Just as the prophet Nathan forced David to convict himself with the parable of the ewe lamb, Isaiah summons the inhabitants of Jerusalem and Judah to listen to the song and "judge" between Yahweh and his vineyard. Only after the verdict is decreed do they learn that *they* are the vineyard and that it is their actions that will lead to their destruction (Judg 17:6 prefaces the story of a Levite who serves Micah's private shrine and idol). This theme of reversal is found most prominently in the Judges narratives and in such ancient Near Eastern literature as the "Visions of Neferti" from the First Intermediate Period in Egypt. The punishment also reflects penalties for violating covenants that were well known from Israel's dealings with the Assyrians.

POLITICAL MESSAGE

Many of Isaiah's major pronouncements are tied to specific historical events. The nation was in the throes of the Assyrian expansion. Ever since 800 B.C.E., Assyria had been extending its

hegemony westward into Syria-Palestine. As a result, all of the smaller nations of that region were forced into vassalage and compelled to pay tribute and provide soldiers and supplies for the Assyrian war machine. This led to an almost continuous series of revolts by the smaller states, usually at the time when a new Assyrian king came to the throne. Although these revolts were brutally suppressed, they continued to occur on a regular basis. Israel, like the other kingdoms, participated in several of these attempts to throw off the Assyrian political yoke. By the last decades of the eighth century, however, the fate of the northern kingdom was sealed. In 721 B.C.E., Israel was destroyed and its people taken into exile. The invading Assyrian armies also devastated the southern kingdom of Judah and laid siege to Jerusalem on two occasions (701 and 688 B.C.E.). These were desperate times. Despite his repeated use of the phrase "fear not" (Isa 7:4; 10:24; 37:6), Isaiah's message brought little solace to Judah's leaders.

In the 730s, the Egyptians repeatedly encouraged the small vassal states of Syria-Palestine to revolt against Assyria. This was a typical ploy of rival superpowers, which would use smaller border states to weaken their opponents. Along with most of the rest of the Syro-Palestinian states, Israel and Syria formed an alliance. Such a strategy had been successful in the past; for example, Ahab had joined with other states in the mid–ninth century to prevent the Assyrians from controlling their region (see the "Annals of Shalmaneser III," *OTP,* p. 169). By the end of the eighth century, however, Assyrian power had grown much stronger. Moreover, their ruthless use of techniques of psychological warfare, such as massacring whole cities and mutilating prisoners, gave them a decided edge in any conflict.

Because he fears Assyrian reprisal and does not see any marked advantage in joining the rebellious states, Ahaz of Judah refuses to join the coalition of Israel and Syria. The result is what is known as the Syro-Ephraimitic war. Israel and Syria ally themselves against Judah and its king, Ahaz, and initiate hostilities. The crisis that Ahaz and his advisers must face is complex. On the one hand, as an Assyrian colony, Judah has a **treaty** obligation to put down any rebellion against Assyria. On the other hand, as a covenant partner of Israel, Judah has a legal responsibility to support Israel's struggle for freedom. Regardless of whether Judah decides to support Assyria or Israel, it faces dire consequences. If Judah does not join their struggle against Assyria, Israel and Syria will invade. But if Judah joins in their struggle, Assyria most certainly will punish Judah!

The advisers of Ahaz cannot reach a decision. At the prospect of these two very difficult paths, they vacillate in their opinions and shake "as the trees of the forest shake before the wind" (Isa 7:2). The king temporarily closes their deliberations, ostensibly to tour and inspect Jerusalem's defenses. Regardless of which decision Judah makes, there will be an invasion, and Jerusalem must prepare for a siege. But the strategy of recessing the meeting is primarily to offer the deadlocked participants time to negotiate with each other and possibly with Assyria.

Ahaz's tour takes him outside the city away from most of his advisers and gives Isaiah the chance to lobby the king. Isaiah proposes that Judah remain nonaligned in this conflict. A key assumption in Isaiah's argument is the tradition of Jerusalem's inviolability (see Pss 46:5; 48:8). If Jerusalem is impregnable, then Syria and Israel pose no real threat to Judah (Isa 7:1–9).

Another important component of Isaiah's argument is the premonarchic tradition that considers Judah to have only one treaty, its treaty with Yahweh. This covenant with Yahweh originally recognized Yahweh alone as king of Judah. And as Judah's **Divine Warrior** and king, it is Yahweh, not his representative Ahaz, who must provide for and protect the nation. As a last attempt to convince Ahaz to remain neutral, Isaiah announces the verdict of the **Divine Assembly** against Israel and Syria. The Divine Assembly has indicted these nations for attempting to liberate themselves rather than accept Yahweh's plan for them (7:8–9). Yahweh alone is the liberator of the Israelites and only Yahweh can set them free. Assyria is a mighty power but certainly no mightier than Egypt, from whom Yahweh previously delivered Israel.

When Ahaz refuses to ask for a sign that Yahweh will carry out this verdict against Judah's opponents, Isaiah proclaims a sign anyway. He predicts the birth of a child whose name will be Immanuel. On the face of it, this is just another example of an **annunciation**, a birth announcement by a divine representative (see Gen 16:11–12;

Judg 13:3–5). The child's mother is most likely one of Ahaz's wives who has accompanied the king on his inspection tour. This is also a "time-based" prophecy—an unusual and risky thing to do, since a prophet's reputation was based on his veracity. Isaiah predicts that by the time the child is old enough to know the difference between right and wrong (approximately five to thirteen years), Israel and Syria will be destroyed and Judah will be impoverished (Isa 7:13–25). The child's name, Immanuel, which means "God is with us," is a sign that the power behind Assyria is actually Yahweh. Judah should therefore fear the coming of the Lord, not petty kingdoms such as Syria and Israel. Isaiah matches this prediction with a second annunciation, this time predicting the birth and naming of his own son, who will see the destruction of Samaria and Syria before he can say the words "my father" and "my mother" (8:1–4).

The eventual outcome of these events was that Ahaz requested aid from Assyria, and the Assyrians used the opportunity to intervene before the rebellious states had sufficient time to organize their resistance. Judah's hopes of freedom from Assyrian rule were dashed, and it was placed under even more restrictive treaty obligations. Judah also had to pay for Assyria's "help." Its local autonomy was weakened even further, and it had to pay additional tribute. Isaiah's prediction of destruction and impoverishment came true.

END OF THE NORTHERN KINGDOM

The Syro-Ephraimitic war (730s B.C.E.) was symptomatic of the discontent within the entire Assyrian Empire. Additional revolts continued to take place, and eventually the Assyrian emperor, Shalmaneser V, and his successor, Sargon II, decided to make an example of some of the rebels. Israel, once again a leader among the small states, was targeted in 722 B.C.E., and the Assyrian Annals describe its invasion. A year later the capital city of Samaria was captured, and the nation of Israel ceased to exist as an identifiable political entity. Though many refugees escaped to Judah, the Assyrians deported the majority of the survivors, and the tradition of the "ten lost tribes of Israel" was born (2 Kgs 18:9–12). Although these people survived the destruction of their nation, they lost their identity as a separate people. Even the Assyrian rebuilding of Samaria signaled the eradication of Israelite culture, since Sargon II repopulated it with peoples from other parts of the empire, including rebellious Arab tribes.

The effect of this traumatic event on Judah is manifest in the prophets who point to Israel's fate and warn Judah and Jerusalem that they might suffer the same. Some, including the writers of Joshua-Kings, take this as vindication of the Davidic monarchy and its covenant with Yahweh. Israel, which had broken away and perpetuated the **sins of Jeroboam,** had finally been punished (2 Kgs 17:2–18, 21–23). With the Assyrians still a very real threat to their own existence, however, the more likely reaction among the people of Judah was shock, fear, and apprehension for the future.

In this charged atmosphere, Hezekiah succeeded his father, Ahaz, as ruler of Judah. His assessment of the political situation was similar to that of his father, but he is portrayed as a king who is more open to the message of Isaiah. The account of Hezekiah's reign in the book of Kings indicates that, unlike his father, "he did what was right in the sight of the LORD" (2 Kgs 18:3). Among his accomplishments is his attempt to purify the temple in Jerusalem (2 Kgs 18:4–6) by removing images of other gods (including the Nehushtan, the bronze serpent from Moses' day). He also invaded Philistine territory "as far as Gaza" and presumably extended his hegemony over them (2 Kgs 18:8). These actions were in fact a series of political moves defying the Assyrians, who had imposed set boundaries within their provinces and expected acceptance of their religion and their culture throughout Syria-Palestine.

Because the Assyrians were distracted by other, more active rebellions within the empire, they did not initially punish Hezekiah for his defiance. On the other hand, Hezekiah did exercise some caution. For instance, in 711 B.C.E. the Philistine king, Azuri, and his **city-state** of Ashdod organized a revolt at the instigation of the Egyptians. Hezekiah was invited to join the alliance, but like his father before him, he remained neutral. Isaiah may have influenced this decision by performing an unusual **enacted prophecy.** He paraded around the city naked for three years to demonstrate the fate of those who rebel against the Assyrians (Isa 20:3). Given the devastation visited on Ashdod and Gath by Sargon II, Hezekiah's decision was wise. In his annals, Sargon II boasts of stripping Ashdod of its inhabitants, treasury, and gods and of deporting a segment of the people. Isaiah's nakedness could not have more graphically portrayed the condition of war prisoners to his audience.

Symbolic Use of Clothing

Clothing not only served a utilitarian purpose; it also symbolized social status, wealth, power, and gender. Clearly the cut, the style, the decoration, the color, and the quantity of clothing served as social markers that immediately identified a person. Isaiah's symbolic use of clothing is one of many examples in the biblical text, as the following examples show.

Judah's daughter-in-law Tamar is typecast by her fellows while she is wearing a set of "widow's garments," but she is able to transform herself by changing into clothing, including a veil, that identify her as a **prostitute** (Gen 38:14–15).

David's daughter Tamar is known to everyone as "one of the virgin daughters of the king" by her robe with long sleeves (2 Sam 13:18). When she is raped and shamed by her brother Amnon, however, she tears her robe as both a sign of mourning and as a signal of her change of status.

When Elijah designates his successor, he casts his robe over the shoulders of Elisha to signify that he will eventually take up the prophet's tasks (1 Kgs 19:19).

Amos condemns rich landowners who do not return the day laborers' garments according to the law (Exod 22:26–27; Amos 2:8). Without his robe, the laborer sinks to the social level of a slave, just as Isaiah's "naked circuit" portrays the fate of a disobedient people as slavery.

It was inevitable, however, that Hezekiah's attempts to gain a greater measure of political autonomy would bring his small kingdom to the attention of the Assyrians. During the third year of his reign (701 B.C.E.), Sennacherib invaded Judah and ravaged the countryside as part of his general campaign against rebellious nations in Syria-Palestine. Sennacherib's chronicle is filled with a style of boasting typical of Assyrian political propaganda. This style is reflected in the account of Sennacherib's invasion in 2 Kings:

> In the fourteenth year of King Hezekiah, King Sennacherib of Assyria came up against all the fortified cities of Judah and captured them. King Hezekiah of Judah sent to the king of Assyria at Lachish, saying, "I have done wrong; withdraw from me; whatever you impose on me I will bear." The king of Assyria demanded of King Hezekiah of Judah three hundred talents of silver and thirty talents of gold. Hezekiah gave him all the silver that was found in the house of the LORD and in the treasuries of the king's house. (2 Kgs 18:13–15)

> Because Hezekiah of Judah did not submit to my yoke, I laid siege to forty-six of his fortified cities, walled forts, and to the countless villages in their vicinity. I conquered them using earthen ramps and battering rams. . . . I took 200,150 prisoners of war. . . . I imprisoned Hezekiah in Jerusalem like a bird in a cage. . . . Hezekiah, who was overwhelmed by my terror-inspiring splendor, . . . was forced to send me 420 pounds of silver, precious stones . . . and all kinds of valuable treasures. . . . He sent his personal messenger to deliver this tribute and bow down to me. ("Annals of Sennacherib," *OTP*, pp. 178–79)

The savage destruction of many of Judah's cities, including the important border fortress of Lachish (2 Kgs 18:14), forced Hezekiah into a situation in which his only means of saving the kingdom was to pay a huge ransom. This saved the city of Jerusalem from destruction, but this was little solace to the villagers outside its walls. It also contributed to a belief in the inviolability of Jerusalem. Because the city did not fall to the Assyrians, it became easy, at least for those safe behind Jerusalem's walls, to claim that God would not allow the "place where his name dwells" to be destroyed.

The events of the siege of Jerusalem are also described in Isa 36–37. These chapters place the emphasis on the taunting speech of the Assyrian military official and diplomat bearing the title Rabshakeh, or "Chief Cupbearer." Under a truce he stands outside the walls of Jerusalem and negotiates with Hezekiah's officials. The people who have retreated inside the walls for safety strain to hear the negotiations despite the protests of Hezekiah's advisers. To further discomfort the king's men and to add to the tension created by his statements, the Rabshakeh speaks in the Hebrew language so all the people can understand his words (36:11–12). He sarcastically describes Judah's alliance with Egypt to be as worthless as a "broken reed," and he disparages King Hezekiah's decree to have all altars torn down in the shrines and villages outside Jerusalem. Furthermore, he ridicules Judah's lack of soldiers, saying that even if the Assyrian king supplied the horses, Hezekiah could not provide the riders. His final blow comes when he tells them that the Assyrian army is besieging Jerusalem at the behest of Yahweh: "Is it without the LORD that I have come up against this land to destroy it? The LORD said to me, go up against this land, and destroy it" (36:10).

This use of **theodicy** by a foreign diplomat is a powerful but not unusual tactic. Isaiah himself describes Assyria as Yahweh's tool to punish the nation (10:5–11). And in Isa 40–55, which is dated to a later period, it is argued that Yahweh has anointed Cyrus, the Persian king, as the liberator of the exiled people of Judah. The Persian version of this event, recorded on the "Cyrus Cylinder," is yet another theodicy in that it claims that the god of the Babylonians has allowed Cyrus to conquer Babylon:

> Marduk, the ruler of the divine assembly, heard the people of Babylon when they cried out and became angry. Therefore, he and the other members of the divine assembly left the sanctuaries which had been built for them in Babylon. Marduk . . . searched all the lands for a righteous ruler to lead the *akitu* new year procession. He chose Cyrus . . . and anointed him as the ruler of all the earth. . . . Because Marduk . . . was pleased with Cyrus's good deeds and upright heart, he ordered him to march against Babylon. ("Decree of Cyrus," *OTP*, p. 194)

In one last example of such a use of theodicy, in Jer 21:4–10, the prophet Jeremiah condemns Jerusalem's leadership and asserts that God actually "will fight against you [Jerusalem] with outstretched hand and mighty arm."

The second siege event described in Isa 37 is somewhat difficult to separate from the first, although 2 Kgs 18:13–16 contains the additional information that allows us to differentiate between the two events. The episode in Isa 37 appears to be a part of the siege narrative of Isa 36; however, it more directly involves

Yahweh's assurance that Jerusalem shall be saved: "For I will defend this city to save it, for my own sake, and for the sake of my servant David." The narrative is an example of an **apology**, a literary device used to defend an individual, in this case Hezekiah. When Hezekiah prays for Yahweh's assistance, an angel brings a plague that kills 185,000 Assyrians overnight (37:36). Hezekiah's trust in Yahweh thus results in a miraculous deliverance of the city of Jerusalem, as Sennacherib strikes camp and goes home. The narrative ends with a reference to Sennacherib's assassination by his sons (2 Kgs 19:36–37; Isa 37:37–38).

Historians remain intrigued by this account of Jerusalem's deliverance. It is possible that the death of the Assyrian soldiers was the result of a plague; certainly plague in overcrowded army camps was well known in the ancient world. Apart from a story reported by the Greek historian Herodotus, however, there is no evidence to confirm that such a plague struck Sennacherib's army while it was in Palestine. And while the Assyrian chronicles report that Sennacherib's sons assassinated him, there is no reason to connect that event with Isaiah's prophecy.

Since the factuality of Isa 37 cannot be confirmed, it is better to interpret it as a tale based on the tradition of Jerusalem's inviolability. The story thus underscores the belief that Yahweh will protect Jerusalem, especially when its kings put their trust in God. But perpetuating the idea that Jerusalem cannot be destroyed has disastrous consequences. One hundred years later, a mob will nearly kill Jeremiah because he prophesies the destruction of Jerusalem and the temple (Jer 7 and 26) and thereby challenges the veracity of this cherished tradition. But when the Neo-Babylonian king Nebuchadnezzar does destroy Jerusalem along with the temple, it becomes clear that the tradition of Jerusalem's inviolability generated false hopes.

THE REMNANT

Isaiah is particularly harsh in his oracles against the northern kingdom of Israel. This may be the result of the Syro-Ephraimitic war or other tensions between the two kingdoms. Reversing God's covenant promise to Abraham that his descendants would be "as numerous as the stars of heaven and as the sand on the seashore," the prophet declares that only a remnant will return:

> For though your people Israel were like the sand of the sea,
> only a remnant of them will return. (Isa 10:22)

This reversal of the terms of the covenant is reminiscent of the symbolic name of Hosea's child, *Lo-ammi*, "Not My People" (see Hos 1:9), and Isaiah's declaration must have been frightening to both Israel and Judah. Fertility of the land and people had always been a concern, but now the decimation of the population by the rampaging armies of Assyria underscored the impending reality of the death of Israel.

Knowledge and the Fear of the Lord

A common biblical theme is the idea that the fear of the Lord leads to the kind of knowledge that is essential for life (Ps 111:10; Prov 1:7). The association of fear and knowledge is reflected in Job's admission that he did not truly know God until he saw God with his own eyes (Job 42:5–6).

The fear of God is also described as a quality of righteousness:

Abraham justifies his own unethical actions in Gerar because "there is no fear of God in this place" (Gen 20:11).

Jethro encourages Moses to select elders to assist him, saying, "men who fear God are trustworthy" (Exod 18:21).

Samuel describes a just king as one who rules in the fear of God (1 Sam 12:24).

Several proverbs state that the fear of the Lord "is hatred of evil" (Prov 8:13) and brings honor and life (Prov 22:4; 10:27).

Jeremiah claims that Israel's punishment is due to unwillingness to "say in their hearts, 'Let us fear the LORD our God'" (Jer 5:24).

To soften this specter of destruction and to make the case once again for God's faithfulness to those who obey the covenant, Isaiah matches nearly every prediction of destruction with a promise of the restoration of a faithful remnant and the punishment of Judah's enemies (see Isa 10:24–26):

> The surviving remnant of the house of Judah shall again take root downward, and bear fruit upward; for from Jerusalem a remnant shall go out, and from Mount Zion a band of survivors. The zeal of the LORD of hosts will do this. (37:30–32)

Coupled with this is his assurance that a representative of the ruling House of David will lead the remnant. Thus, in 11:1–2, from the ruin of the nation will spring "a shoot from the stump of Jesse" (David's father). From what appears to be a lifeless stump, green shoots will emerge to demonstrate conclusively that the people of the covenant will be restored. The restored ruler will be imbued with Yahweh's wise counsel and will serve as the model for a people who must have the knowledge and fear of Yahweh to survive (11:3). Similarly, the familiar prediction of the "child born for us" in 9:6–7 refers to an idealized Davidic king who, unlike Ahaz, can lead the people while faithfully adhering to the terms of the covenant.

Additional attention will be given later in this volume to the other two sections of the book of Isaiah. Isaiah of Jerusalem apparently ended his activities with the end of Hezekiah's reign (see Isa 38–39) in 687 B.C.E. His message was passed on to a school of his disciples; perhaps those who assist him are mentioned in 8:16. They would keep his message, vocabulary, and style alive and revive it after the exile.

9

THE BOOK OF MICAH

An exact contemporary of Isaiah of Jerusalem, the prophet Micah has a distinctively different perspective on the events during the last three decades of the eighth century B.C.E. and the beginning of the seventh century B.C.E. (Mic 1:1). He lived in Moresheth, about six miles northeast of Lachish in the Shephelah and twenty miles southwest of Jerusalem. Along with Lachish, Adullam, and Mareshah, Moresheth served as a fortified center on the western border of Judah (2 Chr 11:8). Micah's view of the conditions of that period represents the feelings and concerns of the rural farmers and villagers who bore the brunt of the Assyrian army's pillaging. When Shalmaneser III invaded Samaria and the northern kingdom in 724 B.C.E., the armies stripped the land of food and exiled the surviving population. Later, when the people of Jerusalem were bottled up under siege by Sennacherib's army (701 B.C.E.), the rest of Judah's population was subjected to rape, execution, and enslavement as the Assyrian troops once again foraged the countryside for food and supplies. As a result, Micah is sharply critical of the Israelite capital of Samaria and of Judah's capital at Jerusalem. He declares that the kings and priests are "cannibals" (Mic 3:2–3) who have stripped the flesh from the people with taxation and their deceitful and corrupt leadership (3:11). His message emphasizes the terms of the Mosaic **covenant** and condemns the monarchy and the priesthood.

JUDICIAL ORACLES

Micah casts his denunciation of Jerusalem and Samaria and their leadership in the form of a divine lawsuit. Isaiah did a similar thing in his juridical parable, the "Song of the Vineyard" (Isa 5:1–7), but Micah points more specifically to the urban centers as the cause of the peoples' despair and destruction. Their idolatry and foreign alliances have incurred both God's wrath and the heavy hand of the conqueror (Mic 1:15). Just as the invaders have trampled the countryside, so now they will devastate and depopulate the capital cities, which will become "a heap in the open country, a place for planting vineyards" (1:6). When Samaria falls after a prolonged siege to the Assyrians in 721 B.C.E., Micah notes that its once mighty walls "pour down . . . into the valley" (1:6); the path of destruction may be reflected in 1:10–15. As the helpless peasant farmers in neighboring villages attempt to defend their homes, they too are slaughtered or deported. In the wake of such general destruction, the prophet calls on the people to repent and mourn their fate. Like Isaiah (Isa 20:2), the mourners are to strip themselves naked and walk barefoot into exile to the sound of scavenging jackals (Mic 1:8). Their shaved heads will indicate that they are no longer "pampered children" but prisoners of war (1:16; compare Ezek 5:1–4).

Micah's Charges against Judah

Like Hosea (Hos 4:10–15), Micah describes the idolatry of the Israelites as a form of adultery against Yahweh. Israel has **prostituted** herself by worshiping other gods and now, as the city is consumed by fire, the images are smashed or melted down to serve as loot for the Assyrian conquerors.

Large landowners and wealthy individuals prey upon small farmers, seizing their land for debt, squeezing them off their holdings, and depriving them of their covenantal inheritance (Mic 2:1–2). Isaiah makes a similar charge against those who "join house to house, who add field to field" (Isa 5:8). These ravenous, landed gentry will in turn be dispossessed by the Assyrians and thus will be unable to pass their lands on to their heirs (Mic 2:4–5).

Just as Amos previously charged and as Jeremiah will later pronounce (Amos 2:12; Jer 6:14; 8:11), the people of Israel listen only to prophets who proclaim "peace, peace, when there is no peace" (Mic 2:6). The "empty falsehoods" are the only ones acceptable to a blinded people (2:11). These false seers and diviners will be put to shame, covering their lips to hide their disgrace and mourn their fate (compare Ezek 24:17).

The political leaders of Israel are unjust and corrupt. They "hate good and love evil" (Mic 3:2, 9), and the officials and judges take bribes (7:3). This charge, which depicts a world turned upside down, occurs frequently in the **wisdom literature** of the ancient Near East. For example, the "Eloquent Peasant" of ancient Egypt charges that lawmakers "tolerate injustice" (*OTP*, p. 219). The Egyptian considering suicide justifies himself by saying that "everyone chooses evil, everyone rejects the good," (*OTP*, p. 212). The "Babylonian Job" laments that the people only "listen to the wicked" and the wealthy even "steal a beggar's bowl" (*OTP*, p. 226).

Micah condemns corrupt business practices, pointing to "wicked scales and a bag of dishonest weights" (Mic 6:11; compare Amos 8:5–6).

The leaders and people of Israel have "kept the statutes of Omri and all the works of the house of Ahab" (Mic 6:16). Like the phrase **"sins of Jeroboam"** (2 Kgs 13:2; 17:21–23), Micah's "statutes of Omri" signifies the reason for Israel's downfall. Micah thus suggests that the international dealings of the Omride dynasty led to Israel's destruction by bringing it into the Assyrian sphere of influence.

Micah also targets Jerusalem for destruction because of its widespread corruption and self-deception. In Mic 3:12, he repeats his statement that the city will "become a heap of ruins" and adds that Zion, the Temple Mount, "shall be plowed as a field." This harsh message demonstrates just how complete the destruction is to be. A field cannot be plowed or planted until it has been completely cleared of vegetation, stones, and other debris. The clean sweep will clear away the homes as well as their inhabitants, and the Assyrians will then draw upon the benefits of the land that has been forfeited by the disobedient people of Judah. Apparently, this statement stuck in the popular mind, since it is quoted by the elders again in Jeremiah's trial in Jer 26:18. It also inadvertently contributed to the belief in the inviolability of Jerusalem, since it served to show that God had apparently relented in Hezekiah's day and chosen not to destroy the city and temple after all. Thus, when Micah's statement is quoted by the village elders at Jeremiah's trial, they do so in the hope that "the LORD [would] change his mind about the disaster that he had pronounced against them" (Jer 26:19).

In his own day, however, Micah would have witnessed the burning of villages throughout the countryside of Judah and the utter destruction of the nation of Israel. He couples his **lament** that "the faithful have disappeared from the land" (Mic 7:2a) with charges that those who remain "lie in wait for blood" while their "hands are skilled to do evil" (7:2b–3). This world represents a complete reversal of the ideals of the covenant community. Trust between friends is impossible; children treat their parents with contempt; and entire families are at war with each other (7:5–6). There can be no withholding of God's displeasure in the face of such corruption. Familiar images from his village background illustrate the fate of a land without law:

> You shall eat, but not be satisfied . . . you shall put away, but not save. . . . You shall sow, but not reap; you shall tread olives, but not anoint yourselves with oil; you shall tread grapes, but not drink wine. (6:14–15)

RESTORATION

Some scholars suggest that later Judean editors have inserted the passages that describe the restoration of the Davidic monarchy. It is not out of character, however, for a seventh-century prophet to use these themes. One of Micah's most important statements concerns the rise of a new Davidic ruler from Bethlehem (5:2). Such a prophecy serves two purposes. First, it takes the monarchy back to its roots, since this is also David's birthplace. It also removes the taint of "career politician" or "insider" from the monarchy. David did not inherit the throne; instead he had been chosen by God, anointed by the prophet Samuel, and recognized by the civil authorities after the death of Saul's son Ishbaal (2 Sam 5:1–5). Like the idealized figure of David, this new king will be obedient to Yahweh's voice, "feeding the flock" and providing the people with security and peace (Mic 5:4–5; compare Ezek 34:23–24).

Micah's vision of restoration also includes cleansing the nation of all vestiges of foreign worship, including forms of magic employed by incantation priests. There is also to be a general removal of all of the sacred stones, or *massebot*, that had been worshiped for centuries in the Canaanite cities of Gezer, Shechem, Hazor, and Arad. And finally, the worship of Asherah, the mother goddess of Canaanite and Ugaritic religion, is to be eliminated. Her sacred poles and groves are to be cut down and all manifestations of her cult outlawed (Mic 5:12–14).

When Yahweh has removed the evildoers from the land and justice is restored, then the shame that was upon the nation will be removed. The nations of Assyria and Egypt will become desolate and will "stand in fear" of Yahweh (7:8–20). They will be humbled, forced to lick the dust like serpents (see Isa 14:29; Jer 8:17). Like many prophets, therefore, Micah becomes a voice of condemnation in the present but also of hope for a better future. He calls for the people to "walk humbly" with God while they strive to "do justice and love kindness" (Mic 6:8)—all attributes of their covenant obligations. In addition, he assures the people that their God "does not retain his anger forever" for those who form the **remnant** of the faithful (7:18–20).

10

PROPHETIC VOICES OF THE LATE
SEVENTH CENTURY

Because the people and culture of Judah were completely subordinated to Assyrian influences during the long reign of Manasseh (687–642 B.C.E.), there are no surviving prophetic voices from the mid–seventh century. What little is known of this period is recorded in 2 Kgs 21:1–18, which is a litany of the king's crimes and **apostasies** (esp. 21:2–9):

> Manasseh rebuilt the high places, erected altars to Baal, and set up an **Asherah pole.**
>
> He built altars for all the "host of heaven" and set up an image *(pesel)* of Asherah in the Jerusalem temple.
>
> He made his son "pass through fire" and practiced soothsaying and augury (see Nah 3:4).

In contrast, the **Chronicler's** account portrays both Manasseh's religious crimes (2 Chr 33:2–9) and his transformation into a repentant sovereign and reformer (2 Chr 33:10–17). While the **Deuteronomist** has used Manasseh's overt apostasy as a principal cause of Jerusalem's destruction by the Neo-Babylonians, the Chronicler has made a theological decision that reshapes the king's role and character. This may be a response to the length of his reign (fifty-five years), since, for the Chronicler, it would be uncon-scionable for an unrepentant ruler to remain on his throne for so long without experiencing God's wrath. It is unlikely, however, that the story of the penitent Manasseh, who is held captive in Babylon by the Assyrians and in his despair calls on **Yahweh** for deliverance (2 Chr 33:12–13), reflects historical reality.

In any case, in the decades following the pronouncements of Isaiah and Micah, no prophetic voice is heard, or at least recorded. During that time Judah was completely submerged in Assyrian culture and politics. Certainly, there had been other occasions when Israelite culture and religion were threatened with extinction; however, the writer of 1–2 Kings treats this period as a dark age during which the people are led astray by their king Manasseh and the nobility (2 Kgs 21:9). Prophetic activity returns in the latter half of the seventh century during the reign of Josiah (640–609 B.C.E.), which coincides with the decline of the Assyrian Empire. The four short prophetic books contained in this section, Nahum, Zephaniah, Habakkuk, and Obadiah, serve as a bridge to the time of Jeremiah and Ezekiel and the more momentous events of the sixth century.

THE BOOK OF NAHUM

No surviving sources describe the author of the book of Nahum. Even the clan or place-name Elkosh is unknown, although some traditions place it either in Galilee or in the region of Syria. The book also cannot be dated with any precision, although its optimism suggests a date prior to the end of Josiah's reign (609 B.C.E.). The **oracle** predicting the fall of the Assyrian capital city of Nineveh most likely dates between 663 B.C.E., when Ashurbanipal captured the Egyptian city of Thebes (Nah 3:8), and 612 B.C.E., when Nineveh fell to a coalition army led by the Neo-Babylonian king Nabopolassar and his Median allies.

The book of Nahum is unusual for biblical prophecy because it so single-mindedly cheers the defeat of an enemy city. Its tone is based on the theme of Yahweh's jealousy (compare Ezek 8:5): because Assyria attempted to subordinate Yahweh to its own gods, Yahweh's vengeance had been aroused. In revenge, then, all of Nineveh's images and idols would be cast out of its temple (Nah 1:14). Also, the destruction of Nineveh and the Assyrians illustrates the theme that God would avenge the crimes of nations who exploit other peoples (3:4–7).

Yahweh's majesty takes the form of controlling all of the elements of nature. The first appearance of Yahweh as commander of the winds is reminiscent of the **theophanies** of Habakkuk (esp. Hab 3:10) and Job (Job 38:1). The whirlwind or the "Cloud Rider" is a common symbol for divine majesty in Ugaritic epic as well as in the Mesopotamian creation story *Enuma Elish* (see also in Pss 68:4; 104:3):

> Kothar-wa-hasis said: "Listen to me, almighty Ba'al, hear me out, Rider of the Clouds. Now is the time for you to strike. Slay your enemies and eliminate your rivals." ("Stories of Ba'al and Anat," *OTP*, p. 250)

> He [Marduk] brought forth Imhullu "the Evil Wind," the Whirlwind, the Hurricane, the Fourfold Wind, the Sevenfold Wind, the Cyclone, the Matchless Wind. ("The Creation Epic," *ANET*, p. 66)

Yahweh displays divine power over the waters, including rivers, seas, and life-giving rains (Nah 1:4). God's rebuking the flood (as in Isa 50:2 and Ps 104:7) puts him on an epic par with Baal in Ugaritic **myth.** But whereas Baal can only temporarily subdue Yamm, Yahweh's sovereignty is complete. The effect of his "voice" in Nah 1:5 resembles the depiction in Ps 29, which concludes that Yahweh's incomparable power cannot be matched by any other god:

> The voice of the LORD is powerful. . . . The voice of the LORD breaks the cedars; the LORD breaks the cedars of Lebanon. He makes Lebanon skip like a calf. . . . The voice of the LORD flashes forth flames of fire. The voice of the LORD shakes the wilderness. . . . The voice of the LORD causes the oaks to whirl, and strips the forest bare. (Ps 29:3–9)

Nahum's description of Nineveh's destruction in Nah 2 employs images similar to those found in the Assyrian Annals. Heavily armed and massed armies, armored chariots, disconsolate prisoners being taken into exile, and the battering down of gates and palace walls all speak of the total devastation of a formerly great people. With Yahweh against them, they can no longer hope to recover their former glories.

Particularly apt in this passage is the use of the lion metaphor in Nah 2:11–13. The chief deities of Nineveh are Ishtar and the sun god Shamash. Artistic representations of Ishtar often depict her with a lion, and Shamash is portrayed as a winged lion. In addition, the Assyrian king Esarhaddon (680–669 B.C.E.) refers to himself in his Annals (Prism B, *ANET*, p. 289) as a rampant lion, a favorite of the gods, who came to power at their command and was able to vanquish all opposition to his rule. Now, according to Nahum, the lion will have no more cause to roar. Its den will be empty, and the sword will devour the "young lions."

Finally, Nahum taunts the Assyrians by asking, "Are you better than Thebes?" (Nah 3:8). This Egyptian city, also dedicated to a god (Amon), had been captured and destroyed by Ashurbanipal in 663 B.C.E. Lots had been cast (3:10) to distribute its nobility as slaves to the conquerors (a practice also found in Homer's *Iliad* and in Joel 3:3), and its rich palaces had been plundered. Now it is Nineveh's turn. The city is admonished to prepare for a siege (Nah 3:14), but at the same time the people of Nineveh are told that their efforts will not save them. Again using a phrase common in the Assyrian Annals, Nahum tells them that their "shepherds are asleep" (3:18) and their enemies now "clap their hands" over the anticipation of their demise.

> Esarhaddon: "King of Assyria, regent of Babylon, king of Sumer and Akkad, king of the four rims (of the earth), the true shepherd, favorite of the great gods." (Prism B, *ANET*, p. 289)

> Ashurbanipal: "Those peoples which Ashur, Ishtar and the (other) great gods had given to me to be their shepherd and had entrusted into my hands." (Rassam Cylinder, *ANET*, p. 298)

Since no nation or tyrant can remain in power forever, the prophet Nahum may be allowed to gloat over Nineveh's destruction.

The feared Assyrians had at last received the justice they deserved. The use of a **theodicy** in which Yahweh is the force behind Nabopolassar's Babylonian army is typical of Israelite prophecy (compare Isa 45:1–4, as Cyrus captures Babylon). The theodicy demonstrates a God who is both "jealous and avenging" (Nah 1:2) as well as "slow to anger" (1:3). This is especially satisfying to the Israelites, who believe that a just God "never leaves the guilty unpunished." The very graphic descriptions of shields dripping blood and war chariots careening through the streets (2:3–4) must have been pleasing to the people of Judah, who had suffered great devastation themselves at the hands of Assyrian armies.

The nation of Judah, however, could revel in Nineveh's destruction for only a few years. They were quickly swept up in the imperial ambitions of Egypt and Babylonia's new king, Nebuchadnezzar. After a brief period of hopeful rebuilding and national regeneration, the nation fell once again under the control of rulers no less demanding than the Assyrians.

THE BOOK OF ZEPHANIAH

According to Zeph 1:1, the prophecies of Zephaniah date to the reign of Josiah (640–609 B.C.E.). The book contains oracles against idolatry and confirms God's judgment of Judah's sins and those of her neighbors. Even though it is certain that Zephaniah prophesied during the reign of Josiah, it is difficult to reconcile his oracles with the events of Josiah's reign. Because they fiercely condemn Judah's **syncretized** religious practices (see especially 1:18–19), Zephaniah may have been active before Josiah instituted his religious reforms in 621 B.C.E. (2 Kgs 23:1–25). But it could also be argued that Zephaniah's prophecies were part of the reform movement.

Like several other prophets, Zephaniah repeatedly uses the image of the "day of the LORD [Yahweh]" (Zeph 1:8, 14, 18; 2:2). This image is associated with God's judgment of Judah and all nations (1:14–15).

The Day of the LORD

On that day the LORD will punish the host of heaven, and on earth the kings of the earth. (Isa 24:21)

Alas for the day! For the day of the LORD is near, and as destruction from the Almighty it comes. (Joel 1:18)

Alas for you who desire the day of the LORD! Why do you want the day of the LORD? It is darkness, not light. (Amos 5:18)

For the day of the LORD is near against all the nations. As you have done, it shall be done to you; your deeds shall return on your own head. (Obad 1:15)

The great day of the LORD is near, near and hastening fast. . . . That day will be a day of wrath, a day of distress and anguish, a day of ruin and devastation. (Zeph 1:14–15)

The prophet's vision is one of the total annihilation of all creation:

> I will utterly sweep away everything from the face of the earth, says the LORD. I will sweep away humans and animals; I will sweep away the birds of the air and the fish of the sea. I will make the wicked stumble. I will cut off humanity from the face of the earth, says the LORD. (Zeph 1:2–3)

Such massive destruction is reminiscent of the story of the flood in Genesis (Gen 6–9). It may also be influenced by the vision of devastation described in Isaiah's **call** story: "Until cities lie waste without inhabitant, and houses without people, and the land is utterly desolate" (Isa 6:11).

One particularly poignant image in Zephaniah is that of Yahweh searching Jerusalem with a lamp for "those who say in their hearts, 'The LORD will not do good, nor will he do harm'" (Zeph 1:12). The image is a reversal of Ezekiel's vision of the marking of the innocents "who sigh and groan over the abominations" of Jerusalem (Ezek 9:4). Another example of this image is also found in Jeremiah's search for "the one person who acts justly and seeks truth" (Jer 5:1). But again, this later prophet looks for the righteous, not those who are to be punished.

Zephaniah offers little hope for mercy. Like Amos, he leaves only a simple path for those who would survive the destruction:

"Seek the LORD . . . seek righteousness, seek humility" (Zeph 2:3). Zephaniah hints that those who do so *may* be among those who lie "hidden" during the day of God's wrath, although this cannot be guaranteed (compare Amos 5:14–15).

Zephaniah balances this dim hope with the assurance that Judah's foes will also suffer God's judgment. And so, like other prophets, Zephaniah also utters **oracles against the nations.** These oracles graphically describe Yahweh's anger against the enemies of Judah and Israel. The Assyrians are included in this judgment. Assyria's proud boast, "I am and there is no one else" (Zeph 2:15a) will not be left unchallenged. That nation's power and pride will be turned to desolation and loathing: "Everyone who passes by it [Nineveh] hisses and shakes the fist" (2:15b).

Oracles against the Nations

Moab shall become like Sodom and the Ammonites like Gomorrah, a land possessed by nettles and salt pits, and a waste forever. . . . The LORD will be terrible against them; he will shrivel all the gods of the earth. . . . And he will stretch out his hand against the north, and destroy Assyria; and he will make Nineveh a desolation, a dry waste like the desert. (Zeph 2:9, 11, 13)

Woe to you, O Moab! The people of Chemosh have perished, for your sons have been taken captive, and your daughters into captivity. (Jer 48:46)

I will lay open the flank of Moab from the towns on its frontier, the glory of the country. . . . I will give it along with Ammon to the people of the east as a possession. (Ezek 25:9–10)

The woe oracle pronounced against Jerusalem in Zeph 3 may be based on the failure of the people to continue the Deuteronomic reform after Josiah's death in 609 B.C.E. Even though this oracle envisions the destruction of Jerusalem, it also contains a statement of grace for the **remnant.** After the destruction, God will transform the people's speech to "pure speech" (3:9; compare Isa 6:5–7). Purified of the "proudly exultant ones," the nation will now consist of the humble and lowly, who "will pasture and lie down" as Yahweh's flock (Zeph 3:12–13).

The final segment of the book (3:14–20) contains a proclamation of salvation for the people and of the restoration of Jerusalem. This section is out of character with the message in the rest of the book. A comparison of the passage with Isa 40:1–2 suggests that it contains postexilic themes (see also Zech 12:1–9) and is probably a late addition to the text:

> Sing aloud, O daughter Zion; shout, O Israel! Rejoice and exult with all your heart, O daughter Jerusalem! The LORD has taken away the judgments against you, he has turned away your enemies. (Zeph 3:14–15)

> Comfort, O comfort my people, says your God. Speak tenderly to Jerusalem, and cry to her that she has served her term, that her penalty is paid, that she has received from the LORD's hand double for all her sins. (Isa 40:1–2)

THE BOOK OF HABAKKUK

The book of Habakkuk consists of three distinct parts, suggesting that these materials were edited and put in final form by the prophet in the decade or so after Josiah's death in 609. The oracles in Hab 1 can probably be dated to the reign of Jehoiakim and, more specifically, to before 605 B.C.E., when the Chaldean armies of Nebuchadnezzar defeated the Egyptian-Assyrian coalition at the battle of Carchemish. Habakkuk 2 reflects the prophet's familiarity with the Chaldean presence in Judah in the period after 605 and possibly as late as 598 B.C.E.

The first segment of this short book (1:2–2:5) is a theodicy in the form of a litany of the world's ills and the seeming victory of evil: "The wicked surround the righteous—therefore judgment comes forth perverted" (1:4b). Faced with the oppression of the Chaldeans and the misrule of their own king, Jehoiakim, Habakkuk raises the question of how long the people must wait for God to intervene (1:2). God responds to Habakkuk's question with five statements of reassurance and announcements of judgment against people and nations that temporarily prosper through illegal and violent means (2:6–20). These judgments are introduced with the word "woe," or "alas":

> Shall not everyone taunt such people and, with mocking riddles say about them, "Alas for you who heap up what is not your own! How long will you load yourselves with goods taken in pledge?" (2:6)

The book places a high value on the person who can put their hope in the eventual triumph of Yahweh and the people of Judah over their enemies: "If it seems to tarry, wait for it; it will surely come, it will not delay" (2:3b). Because this theme of valuing patience over rash action is found in many **wisdom** pieces from the ancient Near East, it is possible that Habakkuk was influenced by the wisdom tradition.

The Value and Wisdom of Patience

The plans of the diligent lead surely to abundance, but everyone who is hasty comes only to want. (Prov 21:5)

The patience of the godly will not be frustrated. (Sir 16:13)

My children, endure with patience the wrath that has come upon you from God. Your enemy has overtaken you, but you will soon see their destruction and will tread upon their necks. (Bar 4:25)

Thorns and snares are in the way of the perverse; the cautious will keep far from them. (Prov 22:5)

Control your temper, save your life. Do not steer your life with your tongue alone. ("Teachings of Amen-em-ope," *OTP*, p. 280)

Blessed is the man who thinks before he speaks. ("Teachings of Ankhsheshonqy," *OTP*, p. 291)

I wait quietly for the day of calamity to come upon the people who attack us. (Hab 3:16)

The third section of Habakkuk, Hab 3, is a psalm structured much like those in the book of Psalms. It contains a **superscrip-**

tion containing the term *shigionoth* (compare Ps 7), which may indicate that it is a type of **lament.** This portion of Habakkuk is also the only place outside the Psalms in which the rubric *Selah* is found (see its use in Ps 46). The meaning of this term is unknown, but it may be associated with the poem's orchestration or performance by a choir. In addition, the poem's imagery suggests that it was used in a priestly procession or dramatic ritual, since it depicts the marching forth of a **transcendent** Creator to save the people: "In fury you trod the earth, in anger you trampled nations. . . . You trampled the sea with your horses, churning the mighty waters" (Hab 3:12, 15).

Throughout, the poem employs natural phenomena to emphasize Yahweh's transcendent power. As his divine rage is displayed against the sea, the enemy's soldiers are slaughtered (3:13–14). The moon is stopped in its course (compare Josh 10:12–13), and the earth splits open as God treads upon the mountaintops (Hab 3:8–15). The idea of nature trembling at the approach of God is common in the Psalms and the prophets:

> Then the earth reeled and rocked; the foundations also of the mountains trembled and quaked, because he was angry. (Ps 18:7)

> For lo, The LORD is coming out of his place, and will come down and tread upon the high places of the earth. Then the mountains will melt under him and valleys will burst open. (Mic 1:3–4)

THE BOOK OF OBADIAH

This very short prophetic book of just twenty-one verses dates to the period after the repeated Babylonian invasions and final devastation of Judah in 587 B.C.E. Nothing is known about its author, but his rage against Edom at least suggests that he witnessed the perceived betrayal of Judah by a nation that had political and perhaps kinship ties going back to the origin of both nations. The book consists primarily of oracles condemning Edom and the other nations that exploited Judah's weakness by raiding and pillaging its defenseless cities and towns. Following the destruction of the Assyrian Empire in 605, Edom apparently took advantage of the opportunity to occupy a portion of southern Judah. Then, when the Babylonian armies of Nebuchadnezzar besieged Jerusalem during the first two decades of the sixth century, the Edomites either lent a hand to the Babylonians or offered no aid to Judah.

This false treatment from a former ally and friend (see Deut 2:2–6 and 2 Kgs 3:9) is also mentioned in an eighth-century prophetic oracle (Amos 1:11–15). Perhaps a natural rivalry between these two neighboring countries contributed to longstanding tensions and animosities. Whatever its origins, the theme of Edom's betrayal of Judah is consistent with other anti-Edomite literature from this period (see Isa 63:1–6; Jer 49:17–22; Ezek 25:12–16; Joel 3:19). The theme may be related to the legendary struggle between Jacob and Esau in Gen 27:41–45 (see Obad 1:6 for the interchangeability of Esau and Edom). Perhaps the most rabid of these exilic, anti-Edomite statements is Ps 137:7, which calls on God to remember the crimes of the Edomites: "Remember, O LORD, against the Edomites the day of Jerusalem's fall, how they said, 'Tear it down! Tear it down! Down to its foundations!'"

The anti-Edomite tone persists into the Second Temple period. A relatively late account of Zerubbabel's effort to rebuild the temple accuses the Edomites of having destroyed it when the Babylonians captured the city (1 Esd 4:45); this story contradicts 2 Kgs 25:8–12, which blames only the Babylonians for the temple's destruction. Similarly, Jdt 7:8–18 depicts the Edomites and Moabites joining forces with the "Assyrians" of Holofernes to attack the city of Bethulia in Judah. It is likely that this distrust of Edom coincides with the growing hatred of the Herods, who were Idumeans/Edomites (Josephus, *Jewish Antiquities* 14.15.2).

Obadiah bases his call for revenge and the total destruction of Judah's enemies on the law of reciprocity. All nations, not just Judah, must observe the maxim that a people who are not at war should not do violence to their neighbors or gloat over their misery (Obad 1:12). This is especially the case for those who are already in distress because of a catastrophe due to natural or human causes. Thus he confidently states, "As you have done, so shall it be done to you" (1:15). The law of reciprocity is a corollary to the "Golden Rule" found in the New Testament and in the Egyptian wisdom tale of the "A Farmer and the Courts in Egypt."

The Golden Rule

Do to others as you would have them do to you. (Luke 6:31; Matt 7:12)

Follow this teaching: "Do unto others, as you would have others do unto you." ("A Farmer and the Courts in Egypt," *OTP*, p. 219)

Do not do evil to someone and thus encourage another to do evil to you. ("Teachings of Ankhsheshonqy," *OTP*, p. 291)

In retaliation for drinking a cup of celebration on God's "holy hill," Edom will in turn be forced to drink Yahweh's "cup of wrath" (Obad 1:16; see Ps 75:8; Isa 51:17). This will then be followed by a general restoration of Judah's land, from Zarephath of Phoenicia in the north to the "towns of the Negeb" in the south (Obad 1:20). The oracle of restoration contains the familiar image of Yahweh triumphant on Mount Zion (see Isa 30:19–26; 31:4–9; Zeph 3:14–20). The "day of the LORD" will bring justice to the plunderers and the occupation of Edomite, Phoenician, and Philistine territories by the people of Judah (Obad 1:19–20). This reversal of political fortunes is matched by the restoration of Yahweh's name as the Lord of all nations: "Those who have been saved shall go up to Mount Zion to rule Mount Esau; and the kingdom shall be the LORD's" (1:21; compare Ps 22:28).

11

THE BOOK OF JEREMIAH

The book of Jeremiah spans the period from around 622 to shortly after 587 B.C.E. Jeremiah's appearance and message coincide with the years of Josiah's reforms (ca. 622–609 B.C.E.), the turbulent years following his death in 609, and the subjugation of Judah by both Egypt (609–605, 601–598) and Babylon (604–601, 597–538). The book thus reflects the wildly shifting fortunes of the nation, from the brief nationalistic exuberance under Josiah to a desperate search for security as Egypt and Babylon fought for control of Syria-Palestine.

Josiah's death had spelled the end for most of his reforms and the beginning of a new era of submission by Judah to the superpowers. First, after the Assyrians were defeated at the battle of Carchemish in 605 B.C.E., Egypt claimed Palestine. This meant a new master for Judah, Necho II, and the imposition of a puppet king. Josiah's son and immediate successor, Jehoahaz, was taken hostage back to Egypt and his pro-Egyptian brother Eliakim was put on the throne. His status as a servant of the Egyptians was graphically portrayed when his name was changed to Jehoiakim by the pharaoh (2 Kgs 23:34).

In 604 B.C.E., the Babylonian king Nebuchadnezzar wrested Palestine from the Egyptians, and suddenly Jehoiakim found himself a Babylonian vassal (2 Kgs 24:1). Perhaps because of Egyptian promises of aid, Jehoiakim revolted three years later and temporarily enjoyed Egyptian protection. This ended in 598 B.C.E. when Nebuchadnezzar once again invaded Judah and captured Jerusalem. This was the first time the city had fallen to a siege since David's time and must have been a severe blow to those who had believed in the inviolability of the city (see Isa 31:4–5).

During this period, the prophet Jeremiah condemned Jehoiakim's policies (Jer 36) and denounced the reliance of the people of Jerusalem on the temple of **Yahweh** to save them from any threat (Jer 7, 26). After Nebuchadnezzar's successful siege of the city, the son of Jehoiakim, Jehoiachin, was deported to Babylon as a hostage along with a group of Judah's leaders and priests (2 Kgs 24:10–17). The Babylonian king then installed as his puppet king the last of Josiah's sons, Mattaniah, and changed his name to Zedekiah (2 Kgs 24:17).

The book's many shifts in literary style and perspective suggest that it was the combined effort of the prophet Jeremiah, his friend and scribe Baruch, and an unknown editor or editors. The portions of the book that are written in first person probably contain much of the prophet's own words; these sections of the book are quite powerful and demonstrate the emotions of anger, frustration, and great personal loss. In some respects, we can understand Jeremiah's emotions as a mirror of Judah's disintegration as a nation. The third-person accounts are less passionate and allow the reader to step away from the emotional intensity of the other parts of the book. These sections reflect on the reasons for Judah's destruction and offer a **theodicy**—that it is, a righteous God who is punishing the nation. Once the nation's period of purification is complete, the righteous **remnant** may then expect an eventual restoration to their land and fortunes.

The structure of the book is difficult to discern. In any case, the materials do not follow a chronological order. For instance, Jeremiah's temple sermon is found in both Jer 7 and Jer 26, while the immediately succeeding episode, Baruch's mission to the temple, does not appear in the book until Jer 36. This seemingly random placement of events may simply reflect the decisions made by the editors to highlight periods instead of sequence in Jeremiah's narrative. Whatever the reason for the book's structure, it requires the reader to step back and forth through the text in order to maintain a clear sense of the time line.

JEREMIAH'S CALL

Scholars are still debating the actual date of Jeremiah's **call** as a prophet. His statement that he is "only a boy" (1:7) suggests that he is a young adult, perhaps sixteen to eighteen years old. It is likely that he received his call sometime during the reign of Josiah (640–609 B.C.E.) and that he therefore experienced and was influenced by that king's Deuteronomic reform (632–609 B.C.E.). The question of his youth and lack of recognition as a prophet may also explain why Josiah consulted Huldah instead of Jeremiah when the book of the law (generally considered to be Deut 12-26) was "found" during the renovation of the temple (2 Kgs 22:14–20).

The account in Jer 1:1–18 contains all the characteristic elements of call stories, especially those of Moses (Exod 3:2–4:23) and Gideon (Judg 6:11–24). Although there are slight differences between the accounts of Jeremiah's commissioning and those of Moses and Gideon, these can be explained by the unique circumstances of each individual. What is more striking are the obvious parallels between Jeremiah's call and those of earlier leaders; these serve to enhance his authority and legitimize his role as prophet. Jeremiah's call story includes:

A **theophanic** appearance;

A statement by the deity of intention and relationship;

An objection by the candidate and a negative label applied by the candidate to himself;

A transforming action;

An injunction and legal empowerment;

A sign given by the deity to reassure and strengthen the chosen one.

Jeremiah is empowered to speak by the touch of God's hand on his lips (compare Moses, Deut 18:18; Gideon, Judg 6:15; and Isaiah, Isa 6:6–7); in addition, God's commission designates him as Yahweh's prophet. The language used here resembles legal formulas found in royal coronations (Pss 2:7–9; 89:19–37). Since the term "prophet" carries with it the power-by-extension of the god for whom he speaks and acts, Jeremiah is able to wield power usually reserved for kings or gods (Jer 18:7; 31:28).

Jeremiah's transformation is complete when he receives a sign that confirms and reassures him in his mission. In Jeremiah's case, this involves a pair of visions (1:11–13; an almond branch and a boiling pot) and their interpretations (1:14–16) reassuring him of divine protection. Finally, Yahweh symbolically labels Jeremiah "a fortified city, an iron pillar, and bronze walls"; this label denotes his invincibility (1:18).

THE "THREAT FROM THE NORTH"

It was noted above that Jeremiah's ministry began around 620 and continued until the destruction of Jerusalem in 587 B.C.E. It is difficult, however, to identify with certainty the earliest **oracles.** Some have argued that Jeremiah's vision of the boiling pot (1:13–15) alludes to the incursions of Scythian barbarians, who overran this area but did not remain for long. Such a short-lived threat would have discredited Jeremiah, at least temporarily. A number of other references suggest that it was the Babylonians and not the Scythians who were perceived as this northern foe (4:6; 6:1, 22; 10:22; 50:3, 9, 41). While it is conceivable that some other group like the Scythians was originally meant in these passages, these references to an enemy from the north were reinterpreted and made to refer explicitly to Babylon and the Chaldean leader Nebuchadnezzar after the battle of Carchemish.

IMAGE OF JUDGMENT

The call to judgment for the people of Judah is found in an image of foreign kings placing their thrones at the gates of Jerusalem (1:15). This may refer to the manner in which commanders placed their thrones on high ground facing the city gates in order to direct an attack. The gate area, however, was also the traditional place of justice, for decision making, and for the granting of favors by kings and elders. Thus David sat in the gate following the defeat of his son Absalom, reviewing his troops and thanking them for their service (2 Sam 19:8). The heads of Ahab's sons were placed in two heaps on either side of the gate of Samaria as a judgment on his dynasty (2 Kgs 10:8). And when they wanted to pass judgment on the veracity of Micaiah's prophecies, the kings Ahab and Jehoshaphat placed their thrones in the gateway of Samaria (1 Kgs 22:10).

In Jer 1:15, these foreign kings have been called to sit in judgment of Judah's sins, just as previously the kings of Assyria had been sent by God to plunder and destroy Israel (Isa 10:5–6). Yahweh serves as a prosecuting attorney or witness (compare Mic 1:2), making a case against the people in much the same way that parents were required to come to the city gate to testify against prodigal children (Deut 21:18–21). The indictment contains the traditional charges that are made against the people by the prophets and psalmists: **apostasy**, idolatry, and unfaithfulness to the **covenant** (Jer 1:16; Ps 8:32–37; Hos 4:12–13; Zeph 1:4–6).

THE TEMPLE SERMON

The first major event in Jeremiah's career as a prophet is his temple sermon at the beginning of the reign of Jehoiakim (Jer 26:1). The sermon reflects Yahweh's concern over influences brought by Egyptian control of Judah (ca. 609 B.C.E.). While the prophet is aware of the political realities of that time, Jeremiah focuses on the covenant and proper worship practices. Accounts of this event are found in Jer 7 and 26. Jeremiah 7, which is in the first person, highlights the prophet's sermon. Jeremiah 26, on the other hand, is written in the third person and concentrates on the public reaction to Jeremiah's indictment while providing only an abbreviated version of the sermon.

The place where a speech is delivered is always important. At Yahweh's command, Jeremiah stages his confrontation with the Jerusalem leaders at the temple's entrance, which is the physical conduit between secular and sacred space. Since he comes here on a major feast day, his audience will include not only the people of Jerusalem but also persons and officials from all over the kingdom. Standing at this particular place, Jeremiah blocks free movement, and he is thus assured of a crowd.

In his sermon, Jeremiah insists on two points. First, he argues, the physical presence of the temple does not ensure that Jerusalem will not be destroyed. Second, only obedience to the covenant and the stipulations of the Ten Commandments will prevent Yahweh's destruction of Judah and Jerusalem. The framework for this message consists of two opposing slogans: Jeremiah's warning "Amend your ways and your doings" (7:3, 5) and the popular chant "the temple of the LORD" (7:4). The latter was apparently both a ritual utterance and a slogan reassuring the people of Yahweh's protection. As a ritual formula, it may have been used when people entered the temple. As the people push forward to enter the temple, Jeremiah mocks their slogan and declares that no chant will cast a protective spell over them. This can only be the "temple of the LORD" if they obey the covenant.

Jeremiah uses the defunct shrine at Shiloh, about twenty miles north of Jerusalem, as his example. Although it once served as the seat of Yahweh worship (1 Sam 1–4), the Philistines destroyed it because of the unfaithfulness of Eli's sons (1 Sam 2:12–17). No amount of ritual or sacrifice can save them or that place (1 Sam 3:11–14) because, without due respect for Yahweh's covenant, it constitutes "hollow" worship. Like Micah (Mic 6:6–8) in the previous century, Jeremiah decries rote ritual behavior that does not contain the desire to obey Yahweh's covenant (Jer 7:23). This declaration, that sacrifice is worthless without the love **(hesed)** of Yahweh and the covenant, is a familiar prophetic theme.

It is also found in Samuel's confrontation with Saul (1 Sam 15) and in Hosea (Hos 6:6): "For I desire steadfast love [hesed] and not sacrifice, the knowledge of God rather than burnt offerings."

Thus the people of Jerusalem cannot expect the temple to save them, despite previous occasions when the city was been spared (Isa 37). They cannot freely violate every law and then blithely call on Yahweh's name, expecting forgiveness. Yahweh is not blind to their actions (Jer 7:11b) and will abandon them just as he left the people of the northern kingdom to their fate (7:15).

Such an attack on the foundations of their beliefs and upon the icon that they had come to consider their safety net could not go unanswered. Baruch's version of the scene describes an immediate outcry against Jeremiah. A trial is organized on the spot, with the religious establishment serving as his accusers and prosecutors, the king's advisers serving as judges, and "all the people" (a collective phrase meaning the citizens present at the time) serving as a jury (26:7–11).

Once the charges of blasphemy and false prophecy have been leveled against Jeremiah, he stands up to speak in his defense. Jeremiah freely admits that he has "prophesied against this house [the temple] and this city" (26:12–13). He insists, however, that these are Yahweh's words, not his own. If they choose to kill him, they will be shedding "innocent blood," one of the worst crimes an Israelite can commit (Exod 23:7; Deut 19:10–11). He also is invoking **prophetic immunity**, a principle that also applies to royal messengers who may not be blamed for the message they bring from their master (Jer 26:16).

Apparently persuaded by Jeremiah's argument, the officials and the people decide to release Jeremiah. Their decision is further strengthened when elders of the land, regional officials probably in Jerusalem for the feast day, cite the case of Micah, who had also spoken out against the city of Jerusalem in Hezekiah's time (715–687 B.C.E.) and had not been punished (Mic 3:12). Although Jeremiah is somewhat vindicated by this verdict, he is quickly removed from the scene by one of the king's officials, Ahikam the son of Shaphan, in order to prevent any further disturbance.

BARUCH'S MISSION TO THE TEMPLE

Jeremiah's temple sermon created enough of an uproar that the prophet was forced into hiding. As a result, during the fourth year of Jehoiakim's reign (605 B.C.E.), he uses Baruch to deliver once again a scathing denunciation of Jerusalem and its leaders (Jer 36). Jeremiah dictates to Baruch a scroll containing this message (36:4), and the scribe then carries the scroll to the temple on a fast day, when his words will have a large audience, including the leaders from the temple and the palace (36:5–8).

The words of the prophet indict Jehoiakim for choosing to be faithful to one foreign monarch (Necho II of Egypt) and then to another (Nebuchadnezzar of Babylon). Micaiah, the grandson of Shaphan, is the first royal official to hear Baruch's recitation in the chamber of Gemariah, a place open only to officials such as Baruch (36:11). He discusses it with other royal officials who become alarmed (36:16). They order Baruch to retell parts of the story for them before deciding to "report all these words to the king" (36:12–18). They also apprehensively ask him, "Tell us now, how did you write all these words? Was it at his dictation?" (36:17). These questions are part of their official inquiry into the matter, since these royal representatives would need to "certify" that (1) Baruch took the dictation and thus was not the author of the scroll, and (2) that Jeremiah was the prophet who uttered this oracle. (Jeremiah's career and his prophetic standing may have been in question, considering Jerhoiakim's response.) After due deliberation, they report the substance of his story to the king (36:20). Jehoiakim decides to get a second adviser, Jehudi, to reread and perhaps reinterpret the message for him (36:21).

In the presence of the Neo-Babylonian messengers, Jehoiakim haughtily denies Jeremiah's indictment. Using a nearby charcoal brazier, Jehoiakim burns the scroll piece by piece as it is read, thereby denying that its contents are the word of the Lord (36:22–23). Jehoiakim's gesture is as scandalous to the people of Judah who have remained loyal to their covenant with Yahweh as it is convincing to the Babylonian messengers who are present in Jehoiakim's throne room. But since the king does not want to provide the Babylonian messengers with any evidence of his disloyalty to Nebuchadnezzar, no one in the court of Jehoiakim tears off the uniforms that identify them as officials appointed by Nebuchadnezzar. They were not "alarmed, nor did they tear their garments" (36:24). Publicly Judah will remain faithful to its covenant with Nebuchadnezzar, even if it means that it has abrogated its **treaty** with Yahweh. For this crime, Jeremiah sentences Jehoiakim to a shameful death (36:32). Privately, however, the political overtures of Egypt, Jeremiah's indictment, and the stories of Baruch and Jehudi move Jehoiakim to declare Judah's independence from Babylon. By 600 B.C.E., Judah is free. Soon, however, the Neo-Babylonians lay siege to Jerusalem, and Jehoiakim meets his end as the monarch of an independent but embattled state.

ENACTED PROPHECIES

Jeremiah made effective use of physical acts, symbolic gestures, and street theater in presenting his prophecies to the people of Jerusalem. Jeremiah 16–19 contains several of these **enacted prophecies.** Each demonstrates a sense of urgency on the part of the prophet as well as a graphic demonstration of the events to come. An insider's understanding of actions and symbols allows the enacted prophecy to convey a message without a long explanation. Such prophecies serve to shock the audience or to present to them the common sense of the situation.

In Jer 16, the prophet's personal life and his normal emotional reactions are restricted quite severely. He is forbidden to marry and raise a family (16:2–4). The symbolism of this celibacy relates to the fast-approaching doom of the city and its people: celebrations at this time would thus be inappropriate, and it would be cruel to bring children into a world in which they could only experience destruction and pain. Furthermore, it is a reversal of the covenant promise of fertility and the injunction by God to Adam and Eve, Noah, and Abraham to "be fruitful and multiply" (Gen 1:28; 9:1; 17:7).

Jeremiah is further restricted in Jer 16:5–9 from participating in any mourning rituals, even for his parents. He may not gash himself or shave his head, nor may he attend funeral rites in which the dead are memorialized and the living comforted. These actions for an individual death can only serve as a mockery of the approaching death of the whole nation. There will be so many dead that their bodies will lie unburied and unmourned by the few survivors. This charge may be a reflection of the **lament** form found in the Sumerian "Laments for Ur":

> When the storm subsides, bodies lay like broken pots,
> The dead are scattered everywhere. Let the people mourn.
> The walls were breached,
> The main gates are blocked with corpses. Let the people mourn.
> The main streets are choked with dead.
> Bodies fill the streets.
> Where crowds once celebrated festivals bodies lay in every street,
> corpses piled on every road. ("Laments for Ur," *OTP*, p. 236)

Another sort of warning occurs in Jer 18. In this chapter, Jeremiah is instructed to go to the potters' district of the city and to watch a potter work with the clay. While he watches, the prophet sees that the potter has become dissatisfied with his creation and has stopped his work, reworked the clay, and is once again shaping it on his wheel (18:3–4). The explanation that Jeremiah receives of this scene is one that would have been familiar to the people of his day. Not only could they easily picture the potter at his work; they also understood the symbolism of the clay as the nation of Judah and Yahweh as the divine potter. The idea that a god functioned as a creative craftsman is found in both stories and art from the ancient Near East. For instance, in the Atrahasis creation story, Nintu-Mami mixes blood and clay to form humans (*OTP*, pp. 32–33). Similarly, Egyptian tomb paintings depict Queen Hatshepsut being shaped on a potter's wheel by the ram-headed god Khnum. Thus in Jeremiah's story, the pot taking shape on the wheel represents the creation of the nation by God the covenant maker. Because the people have not conformed themselves to the desires of the divine potter, Yahweh will remold the clay and begin again, using the essence of the pot (the righteous remnant) to shape a new vessel/nation.

This is an excellent example of the remnant theme. Although the prophet must warn the people of inevitable punishment because of their failure to obey the stipulations of the covenant, total destruction will not occur. Just as the clay was saved to be used to create a new pot, so too will a remnant of the people be spared in order to restore the nation.

The remnant theme also occurs in Jer 6:9, where the prophet employs the image of a vineyard that has already been harvested, just as Judah has already been devastated by the Babylonian armies. Instead of widows and the poor gleaning the remains of the fruit from the vines, however, it is an angry God who "gleans" a remnant of the people. What makes this image so effective is its express relationship to the law in Deut 24:19–22. As part of their covenant agreement with Yahweh, the Israelites were required to leave a portion of the harvest for "the alien, the orphan, and the widow." These protected classes were a metaphor for Israel itself. God provided for the nation, one of the weakest in the ancient Near East, and the nation in turn was expected to care for the weak within their community. Jeremiah's message apparently fell on deaf ears, and this is the basis of God's wrath (see Jer 6:10). The act of gleaning becomes an expression of God's determination to gather all the people into the "basket" of the exile, just as a hungry widow reaches to break off a bunch of grapes. Those gathered in this final pass through the city become the remnant from which God may restore the nation.

Jeremiah's use of enacted prophecies continues in Jer 19 with an **execration ritual**. This public denunciation, similar to the curses found on Egyptian incantation bowls denouncing one's enemies, provided an opportunity for the prophet to challenge the temple establishment and make the point that Yahweh had condemned the temple and the city of Jerusalem. He purchases a pottery vessel and then marches in an informal procession, picking up witnesses and supporters along the way, to the Potsherd Gate. Here he lists a bill of particulars of the people's sins: idolatry, the shedding of innocent blood, and sacrifice of children. Jeremiah then describes the utter devastation of the city and its population: "everyone who passes by it will be horrified and will hiss because of all its disasters" (19:8; Zeph 2:15).

Then, to enact the curse, Jeremiah smashes the pot within the gate and declares that Yahweh will "break this people and this city, as one breaks a potter's vessel, so that it can never be mended" (Jer 19:11). The curse is horrible enough, but to smash the pot in a gate, a place of law and judgment, makes this act a living reality for the people who witness it.

Such a challenge cannot not be left unanswered. Pashhur, one of the chief officials of the temple, arrests Jeremiah and has him placed in the stocks (20:2). This is an attempt to silence Jeremiah by humiliating him. The comic posture of someone in the stocks was an easy thing to ridicule. Pashhur hopes that Jeremiah's credibility and that of his prophecies will be damaged along with his pride.

Certainly it angers Jeremiah, and he calls on Yahweh to take revenge on his enemies (20:12), as he did when his own neighbors from Anathoth plotted against him (11:18–12:6). He questions why the wicked are allowed to prosper and to mislead the people. Jeremiah also questions himself, cursing his own birth (20:14) and the task that has brought him to this fate. He also acknowledges, however, that even if he wished to keep silent and thereby stop his persecutors, he cannot. He feels an inner compulsion to speak that cannot be denied:

> If I say, "I will not mention him, or speak in his name," then within me there is something like a burning fire shut up in my bones; I am weary with holding it in and I cannot. (20:9)

COGNITIVE DISSONANCE AND OPPOSITION TO JEREMIAH'S MESSAGE

In the period between 597 and 587 B.C.E., Jeremiah and the people, both those who remained in Judah and those who were in exile in Babylonia, had to cope with conflicting prophetic voices. While Jeremiah continued to warn of the ultimate destruction of Jerusalem, other prophets and officials were speaking of a quick end to the exile; a return of Jehoiachin, the people, and the sacred objects taken from the temple; and divine retribution against the

Neo-Babylonians (28:3–4). This more optimistic message was much more pleasing to the people than Jeremiah's words of doom.

The most dangerous of these opponents was Hananiah, a prophet from Gibeon. Confronting Jeremiah in the temple in the presence of the priests, Hananiah predicts that within two years the exiles will return and Babylon's power will be broken (28:1–4). Such a diametrically opposed position forces Jeremiah to respond. He first expresses the hope that Hananiah's message will come true, but he then argues that peace has never been a part of prophetic speech: "The prophets who preceded you and me from ancient times prophesied war, famine, and pestilence against many countries and great kingdoms" (28:8).

In this way, Jeremiah explains the role of the prophet. Prophets were to warn the people and their leaders when they strayed from the covenant. They were to warn of the righteous anger of Yahweh and present the proper course that would bring the people back into compliance with their obligations to their God. Peace, however, was not part of the usual prophetic message because it implied two things: (1) an end to current troubles and (2) that the people deserved to have Yahweh intervene to end these troubles. All Jeremiah can do therefore is fall back on the adage that the "true prophet" is the one whose words come true:

> As for the prophet who prophecies peace, when the word of
> that prophet comes true, then it will be known that the LORD
> has truly sent the prophet. (28:9)

Faced with such **cognitive dissonance,** Hananiah performs a physical act to gain the advantage. He breaks a wooden yoke (28:10), which Jeremiah has been wearing around his neck to signify that the people must submit to the yoke of Babylon and thus to Yahweh's will (see 27:2–8). By breaking the yoke, Hananiah negates Jeremiah's message and proclaims that Yahweh intends to "break the yoke of King Nebuchadnezzar" within two years (28:11).

Temporarily defeated, Jeremiah leaves. When he later receives a new revelation from Yahweh, he returns to confront Hananiah with a new symbol of submission—an iron yoke. The wooden yoke may have been broken, but Yahweh has forged an even stronger restraint to hold his people in submission to Babylon (28:12–14). Furthermore, the false message must be discredited and the dissonance ended. Thus Jeremiah predicts the death of Hananiah; the narrator notes that Hananiah died that same year (28:16–17).

There are also voices of dissension among the exiles (29:8). Jeremiah deals with these voices of false hope by writing a letter to the exilic community (29:4–7). First, he discredits any idea that the exile will be over soon. Yahweh's plan provides for a seventy-year period, during which the people must seek the Lord "with all their hearts" before they are returned to their land (29:10–14).

Jeremiah also removes the limits on worship that were placed on the people by the reforms of Hezekiah and Josiah. They no longer have to be in Judah or Jerusalem to worship or to have their prayers heard. Yahweh is not just a local god. The people may worship Yahweh in exile, even without the temple priesthood to direct them. This is a new opportunity for the people, and it sets the stage for the development of **Diaspora Judaism** in the next two centuries.

THE FINAL DAYS OF JERUSALEM

After nearly ten years of relative peace, Egypt lures Zedekiah into revolting against the Neo-Babylonians. Resolving to eliminate this troublesome kingdom, Nebuchadnezzar once again besieges Jerusalem. During these desperate days, Zedekiah sends messengers to Jeremiah to see if Yahweh will intervene to save the city (21:1–2). The prophet can offer no consolation. He warns that Yahweh, the **Divine Warrior**, will fight with the Babylonians against the city and its people will be slaughtered without mercy (21:4–7).

There is only one way to save their lives. They must surrender to Babylon:

> Those who stay in this city shall die . . . but those who go out and surrender to the Chaldeans . . . shall have their lives as a prize of war. (21:9)

Such a message must have shocked the king and his advisers, and it is no wonder that they imprison Jeremiah in a dry cistern to prevent his totally demoralizing the city's defenders (38:4–6).

Eventually, Zedekiah releases Jeremiah and in a private interview asks him again for some ray of hope. After eliciting an oath from the king that he will not be killed for speaking disturbing words, Jeremiah repeats his message that surrender to the Babylonians is the only chance for survival (38:16–23). The king places Jeremiah under house arrest, and there he remains until the fall of the city (38:28).

With the fall of the city only days away, Jeremiah engages in one last symbolic act when he receives word that one of his relatives has died. Although it is kinship right and duty to purchase the man's fields and keep them within the family (32:6–8), real estate at this point is totally worthless, since the people are about to be taken into exile. Jeremiah buys the land anyway. Weighing out the money and signing and sealing a deed before witnesses (32:9–10), Jeremiah performs an act that evokes the early days of Yahweh's covenant with Abraham. Just as Abraham established his stake in the promised land by purchasing the cave of Machpelah (Gen 23), now Jeremiah preserves a title to the land for future generations. He gives the copies of the documents to Baruch in front of witnesses and charges him to "put them in an earthenware jar, in order that they may last for a long time" (Jer 32:11–14). This assures the people that when the Lord's plan is fulfilled and they have returned from exile, this deed to the promised land will serve as their legal claim to its ownership.

Jeremiah also provides oracles of restoration and return just before the fall of the city. In Jer 31, he describes a future end to the exile and a reversal of the current destructive times (31:27–28). The issue of individual responsibility and the casting of blame for the exile is also addressed here (31:29–30; compare Ezek 18). The exiles must recognize they are not paying for the sins of their ancestors but for their own. The new covenant envisioned by the prophet is an internal one:

> I will put my law within them, and I will write it on their hearts; and I will be their God, and they will be my people. No longer shall they teach one another, or say to each other,

"Know the LORD," for they shall all know me, from the least
to the greatest. (Jer 31:33b–34)

I will give them one heart, and put a new spirit within them; I
will remove the heart of stone from their flesh and give them
a heart of flesh. (Ezek 11:19)

When the city of Jerusalem falls to the Neo-Babylonian army,
the royal court is dissolved. Zedekiah is forced to watch his children being executed and then is blinded before being taken into
exile (2 Kgs 25:7). The monarchy of Judah has effectively ended,
although Jehoiachin will live on as a king in exile (2 Kgs
25:27–30). The Babylonians appoint a non-Davidic official,
Gedaliah, as governor, but he is assassinated after only a short time
in office (2 Kgs 25:22–26). His assassins flee to Egypt, taking Jeremiah with them. Thus ends the career of a prophet whose work
spanned the period from the glorious expectations of Josiah's
nationalist movement to the depths of despair as Judah meets its
fate at the hands of Nebuchadnezzar.

12

THE BOOK OF EZEKIEL

Social context is a key to understanding the message of the prophet Ezekiel, who was taken into exile in 597 B.C.E. along with Jehoiachin, the royal family, and many of the chief priests. Ezekiel's message reflects his continuing interest in Jerusalem and its temple priesthood; but as one of the exiles in Babylonia, he must also deal with their fears and concerns. Like many other prophets, Ezekiel's message is divided into two parts, judgment and restoration.

Prophetic compulsion forces Ezekiel to speak the message given to him by God. But this is initially a selective message. Unlike other prophets, he is not allowed to "reprove" the people and thus give them a sense of hope in God's willingness to set aside their punishment once again. He is only able to speak words of "lamentation and mourning and woe" (Ezek 3:10) until the second fall of Jerusalem in 587 B.C.E. God immediately silences any other ideas (3:26). Then, after the destruction of Judah's capital, Ezekiel is released from this "selective compulsion" and can begin to assure the exiles of the merciful intentions of **Yahweh**. Once the people have been purged, they will be returned to their homeland, purified, and restored as God's covenantal nation (36:24–25).

The principal theme in the book is the "presence of Yahweh." In Ezek 10, the departure of God's "glory" from the temple will signal the doom of the nation, and the return of God's "glory" to the temple will mark the climax of Ezekiel's vision of restoration in Ezek 40–48. The theme of Yahweh's presence is also implicit in the use of a recognition formula throughout the book of Ezekiel. This formula is used sporadically elsewhere in the OT/HB (1 Kgs 20:13; Isa 49:23; Joel 3:17), but in Ezekiel it is a recurring refrain. The prophet uses the phrase "and they shall know that I am the LORD" over eighty times (see Ezek 6:10; 12:15; 20:26; 32:15; 39:6). In each instance, God declares that he is about to make manifest his divine power and demonstrates the ability to control chaos and exert total dominion over all creation. As a result, God has established the **covenant** with Israel and given laws and decrees that govern the actions of Israel and, by extension, all other nations (compare Deut 10:12–22).

EZEKIEL'S CALL

Although the story of Ezekiel's **call** evokes images of those of Moses, Isaiah, and Jeremiah, it has its own very distinctive character. Perhaps most important is its sense of mystery. There is nothing **anthropomorphic** in this **theophany**. Whenever the prophet has to speak of God's appearance, he uses a qualifying phrase, "in the likeness of" or "something like," so that he does not have to describe Yahweh in human terms. This creates a majesty similar to Isaiah's temple filled with smoke (Isa 6:4). This sense of majesty is enhanced by Yahweh's addressing Ezekiel as "son of man," a phrase that has the connotation "mortal." In this way a clear distinction is drawn between the human and the divine.

The sense of Yahweh's glory as a separate, roving aspect of the deity can be identified in this scene. Instead of being a fixed being (like the seated figure in Isa 6:1), Ezekiel's vision of God is one of ever-changing motion ("wherever the spirit would go"—Ezek 1:12), which may imply the immediacy of action that is about to occur. Certainly, it would make it more difficult to determine the extent of Yahweh's glory or the degree of power that was behind all of this movement (see especially 1:12–28).

As is the case in other call stories, Ezekiel is confronted with a vision of God and is called to serve as a spokesperson. His task will not be an easy one, but unlike Isaiah and Jeremiah, he does not make a spoken demurral. Ezekiel's reaction demonstrates rather his fear and respect for divine power (1:28). Instead of making any excuses for why he cannot serve, he obediently consumes the scroll presented to him (2:9–3:3). This is a similar gesture to Isaiah's lips being purified and Jeremiah's mouth being touched as a means of empowering them to speak God's word. Once Ezekiel has eaten the scroll, however, he remains mute for seven days before taking up his task. For this amount of time, he sits "stunned" among the exiles (3:15). This, in itself, suggests the magnitude of the message and perhaps his reluctance to assume the prophetic mantle.

Also contained in this narrative is an image of prophetic responsibility. Ezekiel is portrayed as a "guard" or "sentry" whose task is to cry out an alarm when an army approaches (3:17–21). If Ezekiel fails to carry out this task, he himself will be condemned for failing to warn the people. In this case, as previously (see Isa 10), the imminent danger faced by the people is the anger of Yahweh and God's use of the Babylonians to punish Judah. When Ezekiel announces Yahweh's judgment, he then can only shut himself up in his house and await the inevitable. In this sense, Ezekiel differs from other prophets who would announce judgment but retain a hope that God would relent (see Jer 26:19). The hope of being spared ultimate destruction does not appear in Ezekiel.

As has been noted earlier, the attitude that a god is in control of historical events is not limited to Israel; for example, the Mesha Inscription clearly attributes the misfortunes of the kingdom of Moab to the anger of its god Chemosh (*OTP*, p. 158). The idea provides an important key, however, to the purpose of Israelite prophecy. When national disasters occur, the prophets argue that they are a result of the people's violation of their covenant with Yahweh. In addition, since the prophets gave warning that such disasters were about to strike the nation, it was possible to claim that God's willingness to provide a warning was essentially righteous and did not harm his people without cause. This explanation of misfortune as the result of a just and righteous decision by a god is called a **theodicy**. Such explanations were vital to the continued worship of Yahweh. Without this set of beliefs in place, there would be no reason for the Israelites to continue to worship a God who had failed to protect them.

ENACTED PROPHECIES

During the period prior to the final fall of Jerusalem in 587 B.C.E., Ezekiel presented his message in a series of **enacted prophecies,** a form of "street theater." These required him to do symbolic but outrageous acts that drew attention to him and made an indelible impression on his audience. In Ezek 4, the prophet employs a simple strategy to portray Jerusalem's fate. God instructs him to take a clay brick, an item used in the construction of all buildings in Mesopotamia, and inscribe an outline of the city of Jerusalem on it. He then dispenses with his priestly dignity and plays like a child with toy soldiers, besieging his brick/city and showing how it would be destroyed. For a grown man to do this must have caused talk and perhaps raised apprehensions of impending doom for Jerusalem.

Ezekiel's next symbolic action is to lie on his side for an extended period—390 days on his right side and 40 days on his left side. This act symbolizes the number of years that the people of the northern and southern kingdoms respectively will remain in exile (4:4–6). The number forty is particularly significant here, since it is also the number of years the people were condemned to wander in the wilderness following the exodus (Num 14:33). Thus this current exile comes to symbolize a new period of winnowing and transformation. It may also serve as a reminder to the people that even though they are once again sentenced to a period of wilderness purification, that time will come to an end (see Isa 40:1–2) and they will be restored to their land and to their proper relationship with Yahweh.

During the time that Ezekiel endures this painful ordeal, he is required to prepare very scanty meals for himself, demonstrating the starvation faced by the exiles and by those who are to be besieged in Jerusalem (Ezek 4:9–13). At first God commands that these meals be cooked on an "unclean" fire using human dung, but at this point Ezekiel finally protests. As a priest, he had dedicated his life to maintaining a "clean," ritually pure, existence. God relents, allowing him to use animal dung, or conventional fuel, instead (4:14–15).

A third enacted prophecy appears in Ezek 5. In what could be described as another example of street theater, the prophet is told to shave his head and beard. These are normally acts of persons in mourning; alternatively, a shaved head and beard could serve as a sign of humiliation (see 2 Sam 10:4). Ezekiel divides his hair into three piles. Then he chops up one pile with a sword, scatters another in the wind, and throws the third pile in the fire. He takes a few hairs and binds them up in the edges of his robes, signifying that only a few of the people, a **remnant**, will survive (Ezek 5:3). This is such a visually oriented set of actions that it would be most impressive in the open air, where the wind could play its part and the fire and sword could be used effectively. While the act provides no hope for Jerusalem's immediate future, it does hold forth the hope that a few will survive the destruction.

EXPLANATIONS OF JUDGMENT

All of this condemnation and prediction of doom has to be justified, and the visions of Ezekiel provide more than adequate explanation for Yahweh's anger. The most devastating image of disobedience appears in the vision of the abominations in the temple in Ezek 8. This vision follows a pattern that could be expected of a priest who is both intimately familiar with the temple and highly concerned with issues of the proper worship of Yahweh. In an inspection tour that takes him from the outer court to the inner court, he sees the total defilement of the temple, from one end to the other.

The vision begins when Ezekiel is cast into a trance while sitting with the elders in exile. He is dragged through the air by his hair back to Jerusalem and returned to earth in front of the temple. He is unable to enter by the gate, however, because of an abhorrent "image of jealousy" (probably an idol; see the "jealous God" language in Exod 20:4–5), which blocked his way. Instead he is instructed to go to a wall where a hole appears and tunnel his way into the building. He emerges in a chamber whose walls are covered with pictures of other gods and their symbols. The worst thing about this, however, is the presence of the **seventy elders**, who have previously always appeared in positive contexts representing the people's acceptance of the covenant (Exod 24:9–10). In this case, however, they are burning incense and worshiping these other gods (Ezek 8:10–12). Their presence and actions represent the entire nation's idolatry, even within Yahweh's temple. Not only is this worship a violation of the covenant; the direct involvement of the seventy elders magnifies the violation, since they are the political descendants of the covenant's original signatories.

The panorama of disobedience continues to unfold as Ezekiel continues his tour of the temple precincts and finds one example after another of idolatry. First, he witnesses a scene in the outer court where a group of women are "weeping for Tammuz" (8:14). Tammuz is the Babylonian god of new growth and fertility, who dies each year during the dry season and who needs the tears of his worshipers in order to be released from the underworld. Judean participation in this weeping ritual thus represents a rejection of Yahweh as the land's source of fertility.

Next, Ezekiel moves to the inner court, between the porch and the altar. There he sees twenty-five men prostrating themselves as they worship the sun. Significantly, this forces them to bow with their backs to the altar and the holy of holies (8:16), a sign of disrespect for Yahweh. These abominations form the basis for Yahweh's decision to abandon the temple in Jerusalem in Ezek 10. Once again the image of Yahweh's glory appears, again in motion but this time departing the sacred precinct. The glory fills the temple (compare Isa 6:1) one last time (Ezek 10:4) and then is carried away amidst clouds and fire in a chariot drawn by cherubim (10:6–19).

Ezekiel 16 provides one other very powerful explanation for Yahweh's decision to abandon the temple and the nation. This oracle contains a familiar parenting image that is often associated with the exodus event (see Hos 11:1–7). In this metaphor, Jerusalem is portrayed as an unwanted female infant who has been left to die (Ezek 16:4–5). Since female infanticide was fairly common in times of famine or among impoverished families, this would have been a familiar, if horrifying, idea to Ezekiel's audience. Yahweh takes pity on the abandoned child, adopts her, and provides for all of her needs (16:6b–7).

When the girl grows up, God marries her and provides her with rich robes and jewelry (16:8–14). The new bride, however, is not satisfied and seeks out the favor of other lovers/gods (16:15). She squanders all that God has given her, including her children, whom she sacrifices to other gods (16:17–22). She symbolizes the nation, which builds **"high places"** (see Hos 4:13) and makes alliances with Egypt instead of trusting Yahweh (Ezek 16:24–26; Isa 30:1–7). For these crimes, Jerusalem will be given into the hands of her enemies so that she becomes a peculiar harlot who pays her lovers instead of receiving payment from them (Ezek 16:33–34). Just as the northern kingdom (the "older sister") and other disobedient sisters, such as Sodom, sinned (16:46–50) and were destroyed, now the "younger sister," whose sins have made her older siblings "appear righteous," must face her judge, who condemns but also eventually forgives (16:60–62).

The opportunity for the survival of a remnant of the people of Judah appears in a vision of seven men (six executioners and a scribe) in Ezek 9. Here, in what is clearly a parallel with the Passover (Exod 12), the men are instructed to pass through the city of Jerusalem. Wherever they find a person mourning the sins of the people, they are to mark that person's forehead with the Hebrew letter *taw* (an X shape). Then, during a second circuit of the city, they are to slay everyone who does not have the mark of innocence. In this way, the righteous are set aside for survival. Even though Yahweh will physically abandon the temple and the city of Jerusalem (Ezek 10), these few will constitute Yahweh's new people. The warning of the "sentinel" has proven true, and the unity between word and action marks an end to one period and the beginning of a new one.

ORACLES AGAINST THE NATIONS

Ezekiel's enacted prophecies and statements of judgment are separated from his visions of restoration and hope (Ezek 33–48) by the oracles against the nations, which compose Ezek 25–32. There may have been an intentional editorial decision to allow the oracles to serve as a transition or buffer between the two parts of Ezekiel's message. In these oracles, Egypt as well as several of the petty states that encircled Judah (Ammon, Moab, Edom, Philistia, and Tyre and Sidon in Phoenicia) are condemned. This is not a **genre** unique to Ezekiel. It also appears in Amos 1:2–2:3, Isa 13–23, and Jer 46–51. In each case, it is unlikely that the foreign nations addressed in the oracles ever actually heard the judgments made against them. More likely, it is the Israelites who are the audience for these prophetic messages, and it may be assumed that they would be pleased to hear that God intends to punish their enemies.

The oracles are arranged according to a geographical pattern (compare Amos 1:3–2:5). Ezekiel looks to the east as he begins the cycle of condemnation starting with Ammon. He then proceeds clockwise, addressing Moab, Edom, Philistia, Tyre, and Sidon in turn. The editors have treated the oracles against Egypt separately, perhaps because of the contrast between its political power and that of the petty states of Syria-Palestine. Although it is not possible to date the oracles with certainty, they are all aware of the fall of Jerusalem in 587 B.C.E.

The Israelites are to see a portion of their own future in the divine retribution against their neighbors. As Ezekiel declares in Ezek 28:24,

> The house of Israel shall no longer find a pricking brier or a piercing thorn among all their neighbors who have treated them with contempt. And they shall know that I am the Lord GOD.

The elimination of foreign threat marks the establishment of a restored Israel. In addition, these examples of divine wrath echo the theme of the recognition formula and function as further proof to the Israelites as well as all nations that Yahweh is indeed the Lord.

Oracles against the Nations

Thus says the LORD: For three transgressions of Tyre, and for four, I will not revoke the punishment; because they delivered entire communities over to Edom, and did not remember the covenant of kinship. So I will send a fire on the wall of Tyre, fire that shall devour its strongholds. (Amos 1:9–10)

See, the LORD is riding on a swift cloud and comes to Egypt; the idols of Egypt will tremble at his presence, and the heart of the Egyptians will melt within them. (Isa 19:1)

Woe to you, O Moab! The people of Chemosh have perished, for your sons have been taken captive, and your daughters into captivity. Yet I will restore the fortunes of Moab in the latter days, says the LORD. (Jer 48:46–47)

Because with unending hostilities the Philistines acted in vengeance, and with malice of heart took revenge in destruction; therefore thus says the Lord GOD, I will stretch out my hand against the Philistines . . . and destroy the rest of the seacoast. I will execute great vengeance on them with wrathful punishments. Then they shall know that I am the LORD, when I lay my vengeance on them. (Ezek 25:15–17)

VISIONS OF RESTORATION

Prior to the fall of Jerusalem, Ezekiel lays the groundwork for the proposition that Judah's sins brought this evil upon itself. He also emphasizes, however, that the punishment will not continue if later generations prove faithful to Yahweh (11:14–21). To do this,

Ezekiel makes two related statements in Ezek 14 and 18. In the first case, he gives a list of three righteous, wise men of the past: Noah, Daniel, and Job. All survived trials because they were righteous, and all were probably non-Israelites. In the primordial era prior to Abraham, Noah survived the flood. Daniel, according to the "Tale of Aqhat," was a wise king in ancient Ugarit who judged his people fairly and was rewarded with a son and heir (this Daniel is not to be confused with the biblical Daniel). And Job of Uz survived a legendary test of afflictions only to rise from the dust heap and regain God's favor. Although earlier tradition held that the righteous could help spare a city from destruction by interceding with God on the city's behalf (Gen 18:17–21; Jer 5:1), Ezekiel now maintains that even if these three exemplary characters were all assembled, they could only save themselves.

Ezekiel further develops this thought in Ezek 18, where he quotes an old proverb, "The fathers eat the sour grapes, but the children's teeth are set on edge" (18:2). The proverb reflects the legal principle of **corporate identity,** by which children may also suffer for the sins of the father. Thus, when Achan stole from the "devoted things" assigned to the *herem* at Jericho (Josh 7:15–27), his entire family was condemned along with him in order to purify the nation of Achan's sin. In this new world of the exile, however, Ezekiel assures the people that they will not have to pay for the sins of their fathers—only "the soul that sins shall die" (Ezek 18:3). This is not an argument for individual responsibility, nor is it the beginning of individualism, a Western concept that would have been incomprehensible to the communally oriented people of the ancient Near East. Rather, Ezekiel's argument applies to the entire exilic community and is an exhortation for them to recognize the purpose of the exile as a period of purification and rededication.

Once the city of Jerusalem had fallen to Nebuchadnezzar's army in 587 B.C.E., Ezekiel was released from his compulsion to speak only words of judgment. From that point on, his new task was to explain what was ahead for the exiles in relation to their God. They were to understand that Yahweh's decision to leave them unprotected was a direct result of their iniquity. The exile was analogous to the time in Egypt, another time when they had lived "among the nations." They would be tested and purged, as in the wilderness period, and then those who measured up to the stipulations of the covenant would once again be brought forth to the land of Israel (20:33-38). When this period of "instruction" was complete, the name of God would be restored as the nations and exiles recognized Yahweh's power to return them to their land (39:25-29). Whatever dishonor had been attached to Yahweh's apparent failure to protect the people in 587 B.C.E. would thereby be vindicated (see Ezek 28-29; 39:1-16).

The prophet envisions a new world in which old injustices, poor leadership by kings and priests, and the very idea of wanting to violate the law and covenant would no longer exist. In his use of the "good shepherd" image in Ezek 34, Ezekiel describes how Yahweh, the owner of the flock, will take it away from the shepherds (kings and priests), who serve only themselves and neglect the sheep. Yahweh is the perfect shepherd, who finds good pasture for the flock during the day and safe haven at night, who cares for the sick and seeks out the strays. Once order has been reestablished, Yahweh will appoint a new shepherd from the line of David who will follow Yahweh's example and properly care for the sheep.

The exilic experience itself makes restoration possible because it is during the exile that the people come to a truer understanding of Yahweh's power and wisdom. As the prophet says, when Yahweh places a "new heart" and a "new spirit" of obedience within them, they will come to understand the purpose of the exile (36:26-32). And the example of a God who allowed the nation to be taken away and then brought them home again will serve to demonstrate to all nations the power of Yahweh (36:22-24; 39:27-28; compare Isa 40:5-26).

For those who can believe only that the exile means the end of everything, Ezekiel relates the vision of the "Valley of Dry Bones" (Ezek 37:1-14). In this oracle, the prophet uses an ancient battlefield to symbolize Israel's covenant relationship with Yahweh. Taken there by the spirit of the Lord, he is asked whether the dry bones of the long-dead warriors could rise and live again. Realizing that this is a question that only Yahweh can answer, Ezekiel simply says, "O Lord GOD, you know" (37:3). At this point God commands him to speak the word of God to the dry bones. As in the first story of creation (Gen 1:1-2:4a), it is the creative word and spirit of God that bring life. As Ezekiel speaks God's word, the bodies rearticulate and take on flesh again. Then God calls on Ezekiel to "prophesy to the breath," or wind. Again, the reference to the divine breath is reminiscent of the stories of creation. In Gen 1, the first sign of order and life within the watery void is the spirit of God passing over the waters. Then again, in the second story of creation, Yahweh "breathed . . . the breath of life" into the body of the first human (Gen 2:7).

It should be noted that this story in Ezekiel, which describes the reanimation of dead bodies, is not the basis for a belief in a general resurrection of the dead in Judaism. It relates to the covenant and how the people's disobedience killed their relationship with Yahweh. Now, when God takes the initiative, a new creation is possible, with the word and the breath reviving a dead nation. Resurrection as a theological concept will not enter Jewish thought until the Hellenistic period (ca. 300–100 B.C.E.) and only appears in the OT/HB in Dan 12:1–2, which dates to the time of Greek and Persian influence on Judaism.

Ezekiel 40–48 contains the prophet's crowning vision of restoration. In great detail, he describes the rebuilt temple, whose grand scale matches the power and majesty of Yahweh's restorative act. The climax of the vision is the reestablishment of the throne of Yahweh (43:7–12) and the return of God's presence to the temple. Since divine blessings are equated with God's presence, the full restoration of the land and the people is not possible without this divine return. When it occurs, the covenant promise of land and children will once again be in effect (47:1–12).

The reality, however, did not match the vision. When in 515 B.C.E. a new temple was finally built, it was only a fraction of the size of Solomon's temple and certainly not as beautifully decorated. Even at that, it had not been constructed immediately after the return of the exiles (Hag 1). The discrepancy between the vision and the reality would be the basis for concerns in the priestly history (1 and 2 Chronicles) and for the reforms of Ezra and Nehemiah in the Persian period. The people would have to wait until the time of Herod the Great (ca. 30 B.C.E.) for a truly magnificent temple to appear once again in Jerusalem. But even that edifice would reflect Herod's political connections with Rome, not Ezekiel's vision.

13

POSTEXILIC PROPHECY

ISAIAH OF THE EXILE (ISAIAH 40–55)

In our introduction to Isaiah of Jerusalem, we noted that the book of Isaiah could be divided into three separate sections that reflect at least three separate time periods. Isaiah 1–39 is usually attributed to Isaiah of Jerusalem (ca. 739–687 B.C.E.), whose message was discussed in connection with the prophets of the eighth century. This chapter on postexilic prophecy will discuss the other two sections, Isa 40–55, which prepares the exiles for return to the land (ca. 540–535 B.C.E.), and Isa 56–66, which reflects the years after the temple is rebuilt (515–500 B.C.E.).

Isaiah 40–55 is often called Second Isaiah. This section probably represents the work of a school of Israelite priests or scholars dedicated to the ideas espoused by Isaiah of Jerusalem. It begins with a **call** to speak words of "comfort" to God's people, a message that clearly was not in the repertoire of the first Isaiah, who had to shock the people of his time with God's harsh judgment. Second Isaiah appears to have been written during the time when the exile is about to come to an end and the people must begin thinking about the return to Judah and Jerusalem. The most spectacular aspect of this change in fortunes is that a God whose people have been vanquished and exiled will accomplish it. Previously, defeat and exile would have been taken as proof that the God of Israel was a failure, no longer worthy of the people's worship. By freeing them from their Babylonian captivity just as he had freed them from their captivity in Egypt, **Yahweh** now proves to the Israelites and to "all flesh" that there is no God but Yahweh. This "new thing" never accomplished by any other god marks Yahweh as supreme and will become the basis, at last, for the formation of the monotheistic belief of the Jews.

Cyrus, the "Anointed"

The physical instrument of liberation for the exiles was the Persian king Cyrus. This monarch had begun his career in 550 B.C.E. by consolidating control over Persia and Media, to the east of the Tigris River. Over the next ten years, he systematically conquered and pacified the northern and western portions of the Chaldean Empire. By the year 542, Cyrus was preparing to take on this final bastion of Neo-Babylonian power. He was aided in this by the dissatisfaction of the Marduk priesthood in Babylon. Nabonidus, Nebuchadnezzar's successor, had deemphasized Marduk's worship in the capital city, refused to participate in the New Year's festival staged by the Marduk priests, and elevated his own patron deity, the moon god Sin, to the position of supreme god of the nation. Nabonidus had also spent a great deal of his time and effort in the areas south of Babylon, especially around the Saudi Arabian city of Teima. This provided ample cause for complaint and unrest within the capital—a condition that was not controlled effectively by Nabonidus's son and coregent, Belshazzar.

To provide legitimacy for his conquest of Babylon, a document was prepared by Cyrus's administration justifying capture of the city and the deposing of Nabonidus:

> Marduk, the ruler of the divine assembly, heard the people of Babylon when they cried out and became angry. . . . Marduk searched all the lands for a righteous ruler to lead the *akitu* New Year procession. He chose Cyrus, the ruler of Anshan, and anointed him as the ruler of all the earth. Because Marduk . . . was pleased with Cyrus's good deeds and upright heart, he ordered him to march against Babylon. ("Decree of Cyrus," *OTP,* p. 194)

This victory decree is a piece of political propaganda and thus must be read carefully. By referring to Nabonidus's crimes against the god Marduk and that god's eventual decision to seek out a champion to liberate his people, Cyrus claims that he is not acting on his own but at the command of the Babylonian god. Cyrus's army is therefore allowed to travel unmolested through the countryside. When Cyrus reaches Babylon, the priests of Marduk open the city's gates so that he can take it with a minimum of fighting.

It is not surprising, then, that as the Persian army approached Babylon, discredited leaders and captive peoples, such as the Israelites, would welcome Cyrus as a savior. Isaiah does this in Isa 45, where he takes the extraordinary step of applying the title "anointed one" (in Hebrew, *mashiyah,* whence the English word **"messiah"**) to this Persian king:

> Thus says the LORD to his anointed, to Cyrus, whose right hand I have grasped to subdue nations before him and strip kings of their robes, to open doors before him—and the gates shall not be closed. . . . So that you may know that it is I, the LORD, the God of Israel, who call you by your name. For the sake of my servant Jacob, and Israel my chosen, I call you by your name, I surname you, though you do no know me. I am the LORD, and there is no other; besides me there is no god. (Isa 45:1–5)

Note the parallels between the two documents. Both Marduk and Yahweh have named Cyrus as their champion, and they each consider him worthy of their favor. Both have given him a victory by "opening doors"—a physical reality, since the priests of Marduk open Babylon's gates.

It may be that the statement in Isa 45 was written after Cyrus had taken the city and issued his victory decree. This would have been typical of persons or groups who were attempting to gain favor with the new ruler and his administration. Certainly, Isaiah's familiarity with the details of the decree suggests at least an adaptation of its text. Moreover, his use of the term "anointed" and his recital of Cyrus's easy victory would have been pleasing to the Persians. Still, the insistence that Yahweh had chosen Cyrus even though the king did not know Yahweh stands in contrast with the statement that Marduk had sought out a ruler who would keep Marduk's religious festivals and honor him as the chief god of Babylon.

Isaiah claims that Yahweh alone is responsible for Cyrus's victory. No other god helped Yahweh, the Creator of the earth and humankind (45:12), for this God is the only divine being: "there is no god besides him" (45:14c). The idols that Cyrus so magnanimously has liberated are simply objects, but it is the God of Israel that has taken steps to save the people (45:16–17). In this way, the anonymous prophet of Isa 40–55 is able to assure his own people that the god responsible for Cyrus's great victory and their liberation was Yahweh, not Marduk.

It does not matter to this prophet that Cyrus is unaware of Yahweh's actions. All that really matters is that the exiles know that God has once again chosen a tool to affect historical events (compare 10:5). What is distinctive about this narrative is the use of the title "anointed," **messiah**, for Cyrus. No other non-Israelite ruler is given this honor, and it stands as a testament to the importance that is placed on this event—a new release from bondage, a new exodus. While Cyrus will not become a new Moses figure, his political stature as the ruler of the largest empire in all of the history of the ancient Near East up to that time underscores the prophet's claim of Yahweh's universal authority. Quite simply, Cyrus's rise to power is God's means of letting all nations know, "from the rising of the sun and from the west, that there is no one besides me; I am the LORD, and there is no other" (45:6).

The Servant Songs In Second Isaiah, four "servant songs" develop
(Isa 42:1–4; an extended **theodicy** of the exile. The identi-
49:1–6; 50:4–9; fication of the "servant" has been a problem
52:13–53:12) for scholars. In some passages, such as 49:3,
Israel is clearly identified as the servant. In other cases, such as 53:2–5, the servant appears to be an individual, or perhaps the prophet himself. The position taken here is that the "servant" represents Israel.

Clearly, if the people are to resume their allegiance to Yahweh and return to their devastated homeland, they must recognize some value in the dislocation and pain caused by the exile. Thus it is not surprising that the prophet closely parallels the exile with the exodus event. Just as the people were purified in the wilderness prior to the conquest of the land, the exiles were purified in Meso-potamia. Now that Jerusalem "has served her term" (40:2), the exiles are free to return to their beloved city.

Still, there were some who were taken into exile, some who were killed in the destruction of Jerusalem, and some few who remained behind. What sense could God or the prophet make of this division? Why did the people have to suffer? The answer comes in a classic theodicy, explaining that the exile was made necessary by the sin of the people who violated the **covenant** with Yahweh. The pain and suffering associated with their period of exile coincides with Yahweh's justice, and the suffering of God's servant Israel (49:3) expiates that sin. With the end of the exile comes a new pur-pose for the servant. Suffering for the sins of the nation (53:3–6) is now at an end, and the servant, despite his "marred appearance," will triumph and astonish kings and nations by returning to the promised land (52:14–15). The prophet assures the people that, as Yahweh's servant, their faith will be vindicated and they will not be put to shame for their belief in their God (50:7–11).

In the midst of rejoicing over the triumph of Yahweh, the ser-vant is given a new, even more important mission. It is not enough that Yahweh's power is demonstrated by the return of the people from exile. They must now become "a light to the nations" to spread the news of Yahweh's power and to require the obeisance of kings and rulers (49:6–7). While this may be a reference to **univer-salism** and a further strengthening of the emerging concept of monotheism, Judaism will not become an evangelistic religion. Conversion has never been one of its tenets, and it is unlikely that this is the message of the prophet here. More likely, the mission is the demonstration of Yahweh's power above that of all other gods, not the enlightenment and conversion of the world's peoples.

Predictive Prophecy   One of the difficult issues in dealing with Isa-iah and other prophets is whether their prophecies were intended to predict future events, including those in the New Testament. The problem is especially acute in our treatment of the servant songs because New Testament writers and many Christian interpreters read 53:3–9 as a prediction of

Jesus' suffering and his role as redemptive savior. It is worth noting, however, that Isa 53 is extremely ambiguous in its description of the servant's suffering. While parallels can be drawn between the suffering of Jesus and the suffering of the servant, the servant songs in Isaiah do not name names or specify when this redemptive suffering is to take place. Quite likely, the servant was understood to have suffered in exile. But the indeterminate nature of this person or group known as the servant allows for multiple interpretations of these passages, and so it is not inappropriate for Christian writers to interpret the passages in light of Jesus' suffering. This is not, however, the only possible interpretation of the servant songs.

Another proof that is given for the validity of predictive prophecy is the passage in Hos 11:1, "out of Egypt I called my son." A careful study of the context shows that the writer was once again retelling the story of early Israel and its **apostasy.** The theme is similarly developed in Jer 2:6–7; 32:21–23; and Dan 9:15. Yet in Matt 2:15–16 the verse in Hosea is cited as a prophecy that is fulfilled by Jesus' birth and sojourn in Egypt.

Such use of OT/HB prophetic speech by the New Testament writers is legitimate, but it must be recognized as an argument made to "insiders." It was designed to reinforce the faith of the early Jewish Christian community and followed the pattern of discourse, common to that time, of citing ancient texts to prove current events were true. The people of ancient Israel believed in a cyclic universe in which similar events continually recurred. Thus Hosea could speak of Israel's origins in the exodus event while at the same time later interpreters could quite legitimately use the prophet's words to bolster their claims about Jesus.

These "insider" arguments are quite satisfactory proof for members of the insider group. It is too much, however, to expect that outsiders would find them completely convincing. In fact, outsiders are very likely to read the passage in question in light of their own interests and come up with an entirely different interpretation. Such a tendency is illustrated by Cyrus's and Isaiah's divergent interpretations of the fall of Babylon. For Cyrus, the fall of Babylon was a sign of Marduk's favor, while for Isaiah it was a sign that Yahweh had appointed Cyrus to free the Jews from their captivity.

In a similar manner, the New Testament writers used the body of prophetic materials from the OT/HB to make the case for their newly established religion. Both practices are valid, but they must be seen for what they are. Insiders must try to understand the positions of outsiders—to develop an appreciation for the positions of others while continuing to hold to their own conclusions. Ultimately, this respect of each side for the other is the basis for peace and harmony in a pluralistic society.

***Response to the
Call to Return***   Despite Second Isaiah's rallying cry to return to Zion, the question that stuck in the minds of most of the exiles was, Why should we leave all that we have created here to go back to Judah? During the sixty years of the exile, they had started businesses, purchased land, and established their families. If they chose to return to their homeland now, they could expect to have to start over in a land that had lain uncultivated for generations. It would have taken persons of real conviction or adventure to make the decision to go back. As it was, the majority chose not to leave. But in a series of waves over a period of nearly a hundred years, perhaps 15 percent of the exiled community did return to Judah.

Who chose to return from exile? Of course, there would have been the political appointees of the Persian government whose job it was to rebuild this area into a taxpaying province. There also would have been persons with a vested interest in the temple and the status associated with the cult community. These priests and their families could expect to play a major role in the revitalized nation, especially since there would be no restoration of the monarchy. Another group likely to make the trek was speculators and opportunists who saw this as a type of land rush in which they could claim large tracts of land and make a fortune. Among these were younger sons who could not inherit their families' property in Mesopotamia and saw the return as their chance for economic independence. Finally, there were those who saw the return as their religious duty to Yahweh and the covenant. Like Isaiah, they envisioned a glorious procession, proclaiming the glory of God from the heights of Zion.

What these people discovered when they arrived must have shocked them. The city of Jerusalem was not only in ruins from Nebuchadnezzar's systematic destruction; it was also overgrown after fifty years of neglect. The few inhabitants of the land had allowed most of the cultivated fields to lie fallow, and the terraced hillsides had crumbled and eroded. In addition, the Samaritans, inhabitants of the former northern kingdom of Israel who had not been taken into exile by the Babylonians, claimed political control over the entire area of Palestine. They were not pleased to see these returnees with their claims to land and political independence from the Samaritan governor's rule.

As a result, the returned exiles focused on the immediate needs of resettlement and devoted their energies to building housing, restoring and planting the fields and terraces, and managing water resources. This not only occupied their time but also exhausted the funds that the Persian government had provided to rebuild their temple. Only the foundation was completed during the first twenty years after the return of the exiles.

THE BOOKS OF HAGGAI AND ZECHARIAH 1–8

In the second year of the reign of the Persian king Darius (518 B.C.E.), the prophets Haggai and Zechariah (Zech 1–8 only) began to urge the people to resume work on the temple in Jerusalem. Haggai uses a negative approach, pointing to crop failures and other natural disasters as evidence of Yahweh's displeasure at the failure of the people to complete this task (Hag 1:9–11). His message follows a pattern set by previous prophets who also proclaimed that famine, war, and natural disaster were signs of God's wrath (compare Hos 2:8–9 and Amos 4:6–11).

Zechariah employs a series of eight night visions, each of which includes a vision, a question, and a response. In his message Yahweh promises that prosperity will return and Zion will be comforted when the temple is rebuilt (Zech 1:16–17). In addition, God will once again dwell in the midst of the chosen people in the "holy land" (Zech 2:12 [2:16 in Heb.]); by the way, this is the only reference in the Hebrew **canon** to Judah as the "holy land."

Both prophets pressure the leadership in Jerusalem to move forward with this construction project. Haggai calls on Zerubbabel— the Persian-appointed governor and possibly a grandson of the last king, Jehoiachin—to take on the mantle of Davidic kingship and, with courage in Yahweh's support, make a decision to help all the people. The prophet calls Zerubbabel Yahweh's signet ring. Because signet rings were used to stamp and certify official documents (Hag 2:23; compare Jer 22:24), this title for Zerubbabel indicates his legitimacy and his right to exercise the power of the office.

Perhaps because Haggai's efforts bore no fruit, Zechariah turned his efforts to influence the high priest Joshua (Jeshua). In his fourth vision, Zechariah describes Joshua "standing before the angel of the LORD, and the satan standing at his right hand to accuse him" (Zech 3:1). It is worth noting that the term "satan" (Hebrew for "adversary") here refers to an angelic being in Yahweh's heavenly court. Like the satan in the book of Job, this angel's function is to bring human sins to God's attention. We may think of him therefore as God's prosecuting attorney.

The sins that are brought to God's attention are represented by Joshua's priestly robes, which signify the sins of the people and the priesthood. Instead of punishing these sins, Yahweh orders that Joshua be given a new, clean set of clothes and a fresh turban (3:3–5). This is followed by the reassurance that obedience to the covenant will ensure Joshua's place as high priest and the priestly community's role in administering the temple and the courts (3:6–7).

At this point, Zechariah uses the image of the "Branch" to signify a messianic figure (3:8) who will restore the temple and the nation under Yahweh's guidance. Comparable uses of the image occur in Isa 4:2 and 11:1 to refer to ideal Davidic rulers. In Zechariah, the Branch will usher in an era of restoration and justice that will also include the return of Yahweh to Zion (Zech 8:2–3) and an ingathering of people from all nations "to seek the LORD of Hosts" (8:21).

Zerubbabel appears not to have accepted either the title of signet ring or Branch. Possibly he feared political repercussions from the Persian government. This would explain the change of reference in Zechariah's second use of "the Branch" in 6:9-15. It appears that this passage, once referring to Zerubbabel, has been changed and the title is being bestowed on Joshua (6:11).

The "Branch"

A shoot shall come out from the stump of Jesse, and a branch shall grow out of his roots. (Isa 11:1)

The days are surely coming, says the LORD, when I will raise up for David a righteous Branch, and he shall reign as king and deal wisely. (Jer 23:5)

Despite the urging of these prophets, Zerubbabel did not act to rebuild the temple in Jerusalem until he received additional funds and a political confirmation from Darius's imperial court. There had been opposition from the "people of the land" (persons who had not been taken in the exile) and from the Samaritan leaders that had further complicated the political situation (Ezra 4:1-6; 5). Once these impediments had been removed through bureaucratic and diplomatic means, Darius gave the order and construction was resumed. Although the temple was in no way as grand as the one envisioned in Ezek 40-48, its completion in 515 B.C.E. (Ezra 6) allowed the resumption of priestly offices and animal sacrifices and the creation of a religious focal point for the returned community in Judah.

ISAIAH OF THE RETURN (ISAIAH 56–66)

When the restoration of the temple was completed in 515 B.C.E., the people of the province of Judah once again had a national shrine that gave tangible proof of the majesty of the God who had released them from exile. The temple became a source of religious identity. The restoration of the temple and the reestablishment of **cultic** worship, however, created new conflicts. With the restoration of the priestly community to serve in the temple complex (Ezra 6:16-18) came restrictions on who could use the temple and its facilities. These regulations were also in place during the First Temple period, and they reflect the purpose and design of temples, which is to restrict access of increasing numbers of people until only a select few, or even just one person (the high priest), were allowed to enter the most sacred precincts of the temple. But the rigid guidelines can also be traced in the Second Temple period to competing challenges between the returning exiles and the "people of the land," descendants of the kingdoms of Judah and Israel who had never been deported (Ezra 4:1–5; 6:6–12).

Eventually, a very detailed set of criteria was established to determine who was a Jew and what privileges one could enjoy, especially within the priesthood. These criteria were primarily based on kinship (Ezra 2:59–63), but they may also have included considerations of gender and physical infirmity. This seems to be a more stringent policy than had existed in the time of Solomon's temple. In the earlier period there would have been less concern about the dangers of cultural assimilation. The postexilic community was ruled by a foreign power (Persia), and thus the restored community exercised stricter regulation over that area which it did still control, the cultic community of priests and worshipers.

The third section of Isaiah, Isa 56–66, reflects the controversies of this period after 515 B.C.E. While it is conceivable that the same person or group responsible for Isa 40–55 composed these chapters as well, this is not certain. For the sake of convenience, this section of Isaiah will be called Third Isaiah

The prophetic voice of Isa 56–66 challenges the restrictions that have been placed on eunuchs and **proselytes** (converts) to enter and make sacrifices in the temple. The sole criterion, other than obedience to the covenant, established by Isaiah is the celebration of the **Sabbath** (56:2–8). This prophet also warns the people about form without faith. Resumed ritual practices, such as fasting, have become a source of contention rather than a means of worship and an expression of humility (58:2–5). The often voiced statement (see Mic 6:6–8; Jas 1:27) that God's interest in ritual is based on proper motivation is once again used here:

> Is not this the fast I choose: to loose the bonds of injustice, to undo the thongs of the yoke, to let the oppressed go free and to break every yoke? Is it not to share your bread with the

hungry, and bring the homeless poor into your house; when
you see the naked to cover them, and not to hide yourself
from your own kin? (Isa 58:6-7)

The period after the return from exile was one of readjustment and
a striving for normalcy. The desire of prophets such as Haggai and
Zechariah to see the temple restored was a way to refocus the people's
attention on the former modes of living in Jerusalem and the covenant they had made with Yahweh. Simply building a new temple,
however, did not eliminate the abuses of power and excesses of
exclusivism that are a part of any institution and its leadership
(59:9-11). Thus the prophet also calls the people to remember the
simplicity of their covenant agreement as well.

Isaiah 56-66 plays some familiar themes, including a song
similar to one of the "servant songs" (49:6-18), in which the returned
exiles shine as a reflection of God's glory and "nations shall come to
your light" as they recognize the power of Yahweh (60:1-3). There is
also a refrain of God's judgment on Edom for its participation in Jerusalem's destruction (63:1-6; compare Obadiah). Such an oracle once
again provides assurance of God's role as judge of the earth. Yet
another of First Isaiah's themes is found in a vision of a purified creation centered on Zion and Jerusalem (65:17-25) and including the
transformation of the earth into a new Eden-like world in which the
wolf, the lamb, and lion may dwell in peace. This functions as the
ultimate expression of proper covenant relationship:

> The wolf shall live with the lamb, the leopard shall lie down
> with the kid, the calf and the lion and the fatling together and
> the little child shall lead them. (11:6)

> The wolf and the lamb shall feed together, the lion shall eat
> straw like the ox. . . . They shall not hurt or destroy on all my
> holy mountain, says the LORD. (65:25)

THE BOOK OF ZECHARIAH 9-14

The final segment of the book of Zechariah continues the
theme of the establishment of a messianic era, which was first

described in the visions of Zech 6–8. This last section, however, appears to have been written by an unknown author and attached to Zechariah during the middle Persian period (ca. 500–425 B.C.E.) by editors of the material. It consists of two oracles that contain many familiar prophetic elements:

> Indictment of foreign nations (Zech 9:1–8; compare Ezek 25–30)

> The use of the image "on that day" (compare Jer 30:8; Hos 1:5; Obad 1:8):

>> On that day the LORD shall shield the inhabitants of Jerusalem so that the feeblest among them on that day shall be like David, and the house of David shall be like God, like the angel of the LORD, at their head (Zech 12:8)

> Condemnation of false prophets (Zech 13:3–6; compare Jer 29:8–9; Ezek 13:9)

Zechariah 9–14 also contains elements of **apocalyptic** style similar to that found in Dan 7–12. Such elements include the vision of the final victory of Yahweh over the earth: "And the LORD will become king over all the earth; on that day the LORD will be one and his name one" (Zech 14:9).

Zechariah 9–11 is the first oracle in this section. It is written primarily in poetry and features a call to return to Jerusalem from exile (see 9:12; 10:6, 10–12; compare Isa 40:2). This portion of Zechariah may also be influenced by the oracle in Ezek 11:14–21, which assures the exiles that they will return home and cleanse the land of all foreign influences and false worship practices:

> Return to the stronghold, O prisoners of hope; today I declare that I will restore you double. (Zech 9:12)

> Speak tenderly to Jerusalem, and cry to her that she has served her term, that her penalty is paid, that she has received from the LORD's hand double for all her sins. (Isa 40:2)

> I will gather you from the peoples, and assemble you out of the countries where you have been scattered, and I will give you the land of Israel. When they come there, they will remove from it all its detestable things and all its abominations. (Ezek 11:17–18)

The vision is also quite a militant image, as the people are transformed into Yahweh's bow against the Greeks (Zech 9:13–14; contrast Hos 1:5). This most likely alludes to the repeated Greek mercenary and allied presence in Syria-Palestine during the fifth century. Ezekiel's reference to the Greeks—by means of the geographical term "Javan" (Ezek 27:13)—perhaps indicates that they had been involved in the politics of Syria-Palestine as early as the sixth century. In Zechariah's time, they were political allies of Egypt and trade rivals of the Persians. Zechariah would therefore see them as an enemy people to be condemned by Yahweh.

The second oracle, in Zech 12–14, is written in prose style and begins with a short prologue (12:1) that clearly sets this section off from Zech 9–11. By contrast with Zech 9–11, which emphasized God's immediate act of aiding the returning exiles, this section contains oracles that begin with the phrase "On that day" and emphasize God's future action. There is a mixture in these chapters of military action and lamentation over the losses incurred during the fighting (12:7–11).

Of particular interest here is the restructuring of the cosmos after a long and devastating struggle in which Jerusalem as well as the nations suffer greatly. The oracle depicts a scenario similar to that of the Babylonian destruction of Jerusalem in 587; this is especially apparent in Zechariah's declaration that Yahweh "will gather all the nations against Jerusalem" (14:2; compare Jer 21:4–6). After this cosmic battle, peace will at last come to Jerusalem, and all the survivors of the nations will come there to worship Yahweh and to keep the Feast of Booths, thus celebrating Yahweh's rule and the restored covenant (Zech 14:16–19). This reflects similar images in earlier prophetic messages of a time when all the nations will be brought to an understanding of Yahweh's power:

> At that time Jerusalem shall be called the throne of the LORD, and all nations shall gather to it, to the presence of the LORD in Jerusalem, and they shall no longer stubbornly follow their own evil will. (Jer 3:17)

> I will gather all the nations and bring them down to the valley of Jehoshaphat, and I will enter into judgment with them

there, on account of my people and my heritage Israel, because
they have scattered them among the nations. (Joel 3:2)

THE BOOK OF MALACHI

Despite the fact that the book of Malachi is the last in the
prophetic corpus of the Christian canon, it probably dates to the
period between 500 and 450 B.C.E. and reflects the activities of
the priestly community immediately after the reconstruction of
the temple in Jerusalem. Authorship is uncertain, since Malachi
is not a personal name but simply means "my messenger," a reference perhaps to the promised messenger of God in Mal 3.

The book consists of six oracles, each following a question-
and-answer format or an instructional theme. This style of discourse is found in Mic 6:6–8 and, in more extended form, in the
Egyptian "Dispute over Suicide" (*OTP*, pp. 208–14) and the "Babylonian Theodicy" (*OTP*, pp. 223–28).

> *Question:* You say, "How have we despised your name?"
>
> *Answer:* By offering polluted food on my altar. (Mal 1:6c–7)
>
> *Question:* Yet you say, "How have we wearied him [the LORD]?"
>
> *Answer:* By saying, "All who do evil are good in the sight of the
> LORD, and he delights in them." (2:17)

Five of the discourses are concerned with the failures of Judah and
the priests to obey the covenant. The sixth, a condemnation of
Edom (Mal 1:3–4), seems out of character, but it may simply
reflect the continued Jewish enmity against Edom during the Persian period of the late sixth and early fifth centuries B.C.E. (compare
Ps 137:7, Obad 1:6–14, 18–21). In Mal 1:6–2:9, the accusations
against the priests are similar to those made by Hos 4:4, 6 and Jer
6:13–14. The writer begins with a proverb categorizing the duties of
a son to his parent (compare Exod 20:12). The proverb evokes
Hosea's poignant statement about unfaithful and forgetful children as well as ancient Near Eastern **wisdom**:

A son honors his father, and servants their master. (Mal 1:6a)

When Israel was a child, I loved him, and out of Egypt I called my son. The more I called them, the more they went from me. (Hos 11:1–2)

Those who do not honor their parents' name are cursed for their evil by Shamash, the divine judge. ("Instructions of Ahiqar," *OTP*, p. 287)

The emphasis on parental concern and filial obedience continues in Mal 2:10–12. Because the people continue to profane the temple by introducing aspects of foreign worship, including that of the "daughter of a foreign god," possibly Asherah, an indignant Yahweh curses them. These unfaithful persons must be "cut off from the tents of Jacob," a metaphor for the community of the faithful (see Jer 30:18), in order to maintain the purity of temple practice and ritual.

The issue of unfaithfulness next leads to a condemnation of divorce. This stands in contrast to the demands made by Ezra and Nehemiah that mixed marriages between Jews and non-Jews be dissolved (Ezra 9:1–10:5; Neh 13:23–30). God forcefully states, "I hate divorce . . . and covering one's garment with violence" (Mal 2:16). In this case, Judah is the husband who by law (Deut 24:1–4) may divorce his wife, and the "wife of his [Judah's] youth" is Yahweh. But in a reversal of the situation in Hos 1–3, it is the idolatry of the husband/Judah that is covered up by rejecting the wife's/God's charges of infidelity/idolatry. Thus the garment, which symbolizes the marriage agreement (see Ezek 16:8), disguises the husband's crimes instead of providing the legal protection due the wife under the covenant.

These metaphors and charges draw attention to the responsibilities of those who should be most cognizant of their duties and of the law. The specific charges against the priests speak of a lack of knowledge, false teachings (Mal 2:7–8), and improper attention to their sacrificial duties: "You bring what has been taken by violence or is lame or sick, and this you bring as your offering!" (1:13). The law explicitly states that sacrificial animals are to be healthy and without blemish (Lev 22:17–25; Deut 15:21), yet these priests think they can cheat God.

The question-and-answer format continues the theme of instruction in Malachi. When the question is asked, "Will anyone rob God?" (Mal 3:9), God's answer is unequivocal: "Yet you are robbing me!" They are cursed for robbing God of the required tithes and offerings (3:8–9). But those who do bring their tithes into the temple storehouse can be assured that Yahweh will reward their faithfulness by giving them abundant harvests and protecting their crops from locusts and other natural calamities (3:10–12; contrast Hag 1:7–11).

Weary of such unfaithful servants, Yahweh resolves to send a messenger to "prepare the way" for the coming of the Lord to the temple and the reestablishment of the covenant (Mal 3:1). An appendix to the book (4:5–6) identifies the messenger as the prophet Elijah. This mysterious figure, who did not die like other mortals (2 Kgs 2:11–12), is an appropriate harbinger of change. A Gospel writer, seeing the coming of a new age, applied this to John the Baptist in Luke 1:17.

The book concludes with the declaration of a day of judgment, when those "who revered the LORD" will be recorded in a "book of remembrance" (compare Dan 12:1) and will be spared when God separates out the righteous from the wicked (Mal 3:16–4:3). Then, in two appendices, the reader is commanded to obey the law as given to Moses, and Elijah is identified as the messenger whose coming will presage the "day of the LORD." These verses serve as a **colophon** to the entire set of prophetic books (see Hos 14:9 for another example of a wisdom colophon).

THE BOOK OF JOEL

Since the unknown author of the book of Joel never mentions the kingdom of Israel by name and seems to be familiar with the cultic practices of the Jerusalem temple, most commentators assign this work to the postexilic period, probably after 400 B.C.E. A reference in Joel 3:6 (4:6 in Heb.) to the slave trade further bolsters this position, since the **cosmopolitan** Persian rule encouraged increasing contacts with Greek merchants. There are sufficient affinities to Amos 1–4 and Isa 13, however, to make a case for an earlier date.

The message of Joel reflects the uncertain existence of the Jewish community in Palestine and emphasizes the Mosaic covenant. Joel shows a clear affinity with Deut 32 in the depiction of Yahweh as righteous judge (Deut 32:3–4), judgment in the form of invasion and famine (Deut 32:23–24), and recompense for injuries caused by Israel's enemies (Deut 32:43). Although Joel mentions none of the other prophets by name, he draws upon well-known covenantal traditions and prophetic themes. He also draws upon his own experience of his world, which is primarily agricultural, and on the growing **apocalyptic** movement. The apocalyptic themes are especially evident in Joel's dire portents of a darkened sky and the "moon turned to blood" (Joel 2:30–32; compare Isa 13:10) and in the gathering of the multitudes of the nations "in the valley of decision" for a final confrontation (Joel 3:11–16 [4:11–16 in Heb.]; compare Isa 13:4–6).

This short prophetic book centers on the "day of the LORD," first symbolized in a locust plague that strips the land like an invading army (Joel 2:1–11; compare Amos 8:9–10). It is possible that this is a mention or a memory of Assyrian or Babylonian invasions of Judah, but it could just as easily represent any invading force, human or insect, that God would send to punish the covenant breakers. In the midst of the devastation, the prophet reminds the people again that it is better to repent than to perform rituals: "rend your hearts and not your clothing" (Joel 2:13a; compare 1 Sam 15:22; Hos 6:6). Joel also uses the day of the Lord as the moment of Judah's restoration, when plenty will replace want and the presence of God will be made manifest in the people's words and hearts (Joel 2:18–32). This pattern of a plea followed by a reassurance of hope and restoration is also found in the Psalms (see Ps 22) and identifies this portion of Joel as a cultic **liturgy**.

Since the world of the postexilic community is so environmentally fragile (see Hag 1:6), a plague of locusts that strips the fields clean can lead to famine and starvation. The community can also be victimized by their neighbors and be sold into slavery, either for debt or because they cannot defend their borders (Joel

3:4–6 [4:4–6 in Heb.]). Into this reality of want and misery, Joel injects a ray of hope in his vision of a newly revived creation in which God's people will fully enjoy the benefits of the covenant promise of land and children:

> O children of Zion, be glad and rejoice in the LORD your God;
> for he has given the early rain for your vindication, he has
> poured down for you abundant rain. . . . The threshing floors
> shall be full of grain, the vats shall overflow with wine and
> oil. (2:23–24)

Joel's apocalyptic language and visions are quite powerful. Among them is a passage that promises salvation to "everyone who calls on the name of the LORD" (2:28–32 [3:1–5 in Heb.]). Acts 2:17–21 quotes this passage from Joel as an example of the last days and final judgment and associates this promise of salvation with Christian ideas of the resurrection of the dead. This understanding of salvation, however, has not yet appeared in the Judaism of Joel's time. For Joel, the promised salvation involves the transformation of this world and the judgment of Judah's enemies (Joel 3:1–8 [4:1–8 in Heb.]). The use of warfare as a means of righting injustice and gaining revenge, also found in Esth 9 and Nah 2, sounds cruel, but it reflects the pain and suffering of an oppressed people that wishes to strike out against its enemies Edom, Phoenicia, and the Philistines (see Ps 137:8–9).

THE BOOK OF JONAH

Although this book is set in the period during which the Assyrian Empire held an iron-fisted control over much of the ancient Near East (850–605 B.C.E.), it was most probably written during the postexilic period, after 500 B.C.E. This date is based partially on the inability to trace the events described in the book to any established historical sources. In addition, the book's development of the theme of universalism seems to address the postexilic tendency to enforce Jewish identity through exclusivistic claims and cultural isolation. The book of Jonah thus represents a minority voice within the biblical tradition, calling for a wider understanding of Yahweh's concerns for creation. The author uses humor and irony to claim that Yahweh is concerned about peoples other than Israel. Jonah's stubborn refusal to serve as Yahweh's prophet to Nineveh becomes a lightning rod attracting God's attention and drawing other people into an awareness of Yahweh's power. The prophet, like many of his people, must also be convinced that there is no such thing as "undeserved" divine forgiveness.

The book of Jonah showcases the principle that Yahweh has the power to control the fate of all peoples, even the sworn enemies of Israel. When God calls Jonah to preach repentance to the people of Nineveh, Jonah refuses to go; indeed, he boards a ship that will take him in the opposite direction. Jonah's reluctance is understandable. It is even possible that Jonah may have thought he was protecting his own people by refusing to save the Assyrians from their destruction at the hands of Yahweh. In any case, there is no good reason why he should want to aid the people who have destroyed the northern kingdom of Israel, devastated the towns and villages of Judah, and repeatedly ravaged every other country in the Near East. Instead, like the seventh-century prophet Nahum (Nah 1:15), he would have probably preferred to declare a celebration for the destruction of the Assyrians.

The story begins with an outrageous mission. God instructs Jonah to go to Nineveh, the hated capital city of the Assyrians, and warn the people of God's coming judgment. This warning would be the same type of message that the Hebrew prophets delivered to their own people (compare Amos 5:14). When God declares, "their wickedness has come up before me," one is reminded of the prelude to the flood in Gen 6 and the concern in Gen 18 about the evil of Sodom and Gomorrah:

> The LORD saw that the wickedness of humankind was great in the earth, and that every inclination of the thoughts of their hearts was only evil continually. (Gen 6:5)

> Then the LORD said, "How great is the outcry against Sodom and Gomorrah and how very grave their sin!" (Gen 18:20)

> Go at once to Nineveh, that great city, and cry out against it; for their wickedness has come up before me. (Jonah 1:2)

God's instruction to Jonah thus resembles other examples of the theme of sparing a righteous **remnant**. As part of God's creation, the Assyrians must be given the opportunity to repent lest God be placed in a situation in which a righteous person is destroyed without warning.

In the story, Jonah resists God's assistance. He flees his country from the port of Joppa, hoping to reach the end of the world, Tarshish in Spain, and thus escape "the presence of the LORD" (Jonah 1:3). When his ship is threatened by a storm, he discovers is that there is no place to hide from Yahweh (compare Job 34:21–22). While all of the sailors madly throw cargo overboard and pray to their own gods, Jonah does nothing. He is asleep in the hold and only comes on deck when the sailors rouse him with their plea to add his prayers to their own. They hope that, by attracting yet another god's attention, they will be able to still the sea before it engulfs them (Jonah 1:5–6). When they take the further step of casting lots to determine the cause of their misfortune (compare Josh 7:16–20), Jonah has to admit the fault is his. The sailors cannot believe anyone could be foolish enough to try to flee from a god, but they take Jonah's advice and cast him into the sea. Then they pray to Yahweh, offer a sacrifice, and take vows. This story thus illustrates the theme of universalism, as these non-Israelites discern the power of the Israelite God (Jonah 1:14–16).

Jonah is in "the belly of the fish" three days before he prays for his release (2:2–9). The fish and the storm function in the story as evidence of God's control over the natural world (1:17; 2:10; see Job 41:1; Ps 104:26). Jonah concludes that the prophetic call is inescapable. Reluctantly he now enters the Assyrian capital city (the penitential prayer in Jonah 2 may have been added later to make Jonah appear more submissive).

The resolution of the drama comes when Jonah enters Nineveh and without much enthusiasm begins to proclaim the message, "Forty days more, and Nineveh shall be overthrown!" (3:4b). Even as he carries out this task, he shows his stubborn and rebellious nature. He walks a full day into the city before saying anything, perhaps hoping to find some corner where no one will hear him (3:4a). The curious thing about this is that the people of this "great city," which required a person three days to walk from one end to the other, immediately believe Yahweh's prophet: "they proclaimed a fast, and everyone, great and small, put on **sack-cloth**" (3:5). Unlike Sodom, which demonstrated that all of its citizens were evil (Gen 19:4), Nineveh's entire population, including the king, demonstrate their contrition and willingness to repent.

Their change is based on the hope that Yahweh may relent and spare the city. It is interesting to note the close parallel between the statement in Jonah 3:9 and the explanation given at the end of Jeremiah's trial for his acquittal and release:

> Who knows? God may relent and change his mind; he may turn from his fierce anger, so that we do not perish. (Jonah 3:9)

> Did he [Hezekiah] not fear the LORD and entreat the favor of the LORD, and did not the LORD change his mind about the disaster that he had pronounced against them? (Jer 26:19)

Clearly, these people recognized the possibility of "changing God's mind," and they were willing to go to extremes to obtain this goal.

Characteristically, Jonah's reaction to being the most successful evangelist in history is extreme displeasure and anger (Jonah 4:1). He complains that God is too kindhearted and prone to forgiveness. The Assyrians have been responsible for terrible acts of destruction against the peoples of the Near East. And now God has forgiven them!

Assyrian Campaign Rhetoric

They put their trust upon their own force while I trusted Ashur, my lord. I caught him [the king of Sidon] like a bird in his mountains and cut off his head. I hung the heads of Sanduarri [of Kundi] and of Abdimilkutte [of Sidon] around the neck of their nobles to demonstrate to the population the power of Ashur, my lord, and paraded through the wide main street of Nineveh with singers (playing on) harps. ("Annals of Esarhaddon," *ANET*, pp. 290–91)

The prophet is so beside himself over this that he asks for God to take his life (4:3). Again the universalism theme, which made it possible for God to be concerned about even the most bloodthirsty people in the ancient world, allows for the righteous to be spared. Jonah, who knows Yahweh, can only be angry with God for relenting. The key to Jonah's stubbornness is found in 4:2, which explains why he initially resisted God's call. He can proclaim Yahweh's loving and forgiving nature to his own people, but Jonah cannot forgive the Assyrians and does not want God to do so either.

The final expression of this theme then comes when Jonah constructs a booth outside the city. As in the case of the storm and the great fish, God demonstrates mastery over all creation, first by causing a bush to grow and providing Jonah with a leafy canopy (4:5–6). Then the Lord of creation sends a worm to destroy the bush and a hot wind to parch his throat and make him faint with the heat (4:7–8). Again, just as he did when Nineveh was spared, Jonah responds with anger at life's unfairness. He would just as soon depart: "It is better for me to die than to live."

God, who teaches him the lesson of concern for all of creation, then condemns Jonah's self-centered philosophy. The prophet's anger has been based not on the death of the plant but on the end of its comfort-giving shade. God then criticizes Jonah's attitude in a typical wisdom statement that emphasizes God's prerogative to exercise judgment:

> You are concerned about the bush, for which you did not labor and which you did not grow; it came into being in a night and perished in a night. And should I not be concerned about Nineveh, that great city, in which there are more than 120,000 persons who do not know their right hand from their left, and also many animals? (4:10–11).

> Justice is the gift of the divine assembly, given to whomever it wills. ("Teachings of Amen-em-ope," *OTP*, p. 280)

> Divine plans are one thing. Human thoughts are another. ("Teaching of Ankhsheshonqy," *OTP*, p. 294)

God corrects the shortsighted prophet's attitude in a way that resembles the speech to Job: "Where were you when I laid the foundation of the earth?" (Job 38:4a). Because Jonah had nothing to do with the creation of the bush or of the people of Nineveh, he has no right to deny the Creator the opportunity to be concerned with them (Jonah 4:10–11). In other words, God asserts sovereignty and compassionate concern for all of creation, a full expression of the universalism theme.

Connection with the Postexilic Period   The members of the exilic community who remained loyal to Yahweh during the exile and in the subsequent postexilic period generally identified their God with themselves and their own country. It was quite easy to identify God as dwelling in Zion and from that seat of power judging the enemies of Judah (Joel 3:17 [4:17 in Heb.]; Zech 8:3). The postexilic prophetic writers surely enjoyed the task of describing how Yahweh will crush their oppressors. Furthermore, the return of the exiles demonstrated that the God of Israel was truly supreme over all other nations and gods.

What is not so pleasing is a portrayal of Yahweh helping their enemies to repent and be delivered from justified destruction. This message would have been difficult to accept in the period of Assyrian control of the Near East. At that point, the people's hopes were kept alive by the impending annihilation of Nineveh and its rulers (Isa 10:12–19). The book of Jonah, however, comes from the postexilic period, when some voices saw the logic within monotheism that if Yahweh is truly the only God, then all peoples were part of Yahweh's creation, even the seemingly unredeemable Assyrians of hated memory. Therefore, they too deserved a chance to accept a message of repentance. In this way, in the postexilic period, as new enemies emerged to oppress the Jews in Jerusalem or the Diaspora, it became possible to pray for the welfare of their enemies as Jeremiah had once suggested (Jer 29:7). If the nations of the earth could be convinced that Yahweh was indeed the all-powerful, universal deity, then their desire to extinguish the light of Judaism might also be set aside.

14

THE HELLENISTIC PERIOD AND THE BOOK OF DANIEL

Although the first half of this prophetic narrative is set in the period of the exile (ca. 597–538 B.C.E.), the book of Daniel's inclusion in the "Writings" section of the Hebrew **canon,** its historical problems, and its writer's use of late Hebrew and Aramaic vocabulary point to composition in the second century B.C.E. Moreover, there are many similarities between the tales of Daniel's trials and the literature of the Maccabean revolt, which occurred in the 160s B.C.E.

LITERARY ANALYSIS

The book of Daniel can be divided into two distinct sections. Daniel 1–6 contain the "Tales of the Young Men," stories about Daniel and his three friends who are brought to Babylon with the first group of exiles in 597 B.C.E. These vivid narratives revolve around their heroic championing of their Jewish identity through their strict adherence to the dietary laws and their staunch championship of the monotheistic injunctions in the covenant—ideas and practices that develop most fully in the exile and postexilic period. In every possible way, Daniel and his companions resist being assimilated into Babylonian culture or accepting any changes in their religious practices even under threat of death. Furthermore, Daniel's ability to interpret dreams reinforces the superiority of **Yahweh** over the gods of Mesopotamia and Persia. This theme of the conflict between gods, which had been developed previously in the contest between Moses and Pharaoh (Exod 7–12) and Elijah's contest on Mount Carmel (1 Kgs 18), acquires new relevance in these stories set in the time of the exile.

The remaining chapters (Dan 7–12) contain **apocalyptic** visions. Apocalyptic literature can be defined as a special type of literature that reveals secrets of the future, knowledge possessed only by God and revealed only to the elect. The visions are usually full of bizarre imagery and cryptic numbers that must be interpreted by angelic beings. The visions of Daniel deal with the eventual triumph of Yahweh over the kings, gods, and angel armies of the Babylonians and Persians. These visions are difficult for modern readers to interpret because they are based on Israelite traditions and the political agenda of the writer at the time they were composed.

The Postexilic Jewish Identity Movement

In order to preserve their cultural identity, the exiles drew upon their covenant traditions and their history to create an identity movement. These religious standards worked to combat assimilation and helped to establish Judaism as a monotheistic faith:

Editing materials from oral tradition and historical and religious annals to create a "canon" of literature;

Use of Hebrew as a liturgical language;

Emphasis on **Sabbath** worship in the absence of temple and sacrificial cult;

Emphasis on circumcision as a ritual of initiation and exclusivism;

Increased emphasis on **ritual purity**, including ritual bathing and dietary laws;

Insistence on **endogamy** as a guard against cultural assimilation and as a basis for membership in the priesthood.

There is no direct relation between the earlier chapters and the apocalyptic visions. Even the sense of chronology is different in the two sections. In addition, linguistic differences make it difficult to determine the authorship of the book: Dan 1:1–2:4a and Dan 8–12 are written in Hebrew, while 2:4b–7:28 is composed in Aramaic. These differences may indicate that different authors were responsible for the Hebrew and Aramaic sections; if so, the two sections were joined because they were both traditions about Daniel. The linguistic differences may also illustrate the use of Hebrew as a **liturgical** language for the introductory and most of the apocalyptic portions of the book.

Because Daniel's visions are written in the style of apocalyptic literature, they have definite characteristics that differentiate them from other prophetic visions. Particularly important here is the fact that prophets wrote and spoke in their own names while apocalypticists used the authority attached to the name of an ancient hero or prophet as their pseudonym. In addition, the sense of time is different between these two groups. Prophets believed that God worked within history while apocalypticists believed that this world had become corrupt and that God's deliverance would come outside history with a new creation. Thus it can be said that prophecy was an original and creative movement, setting a standard for the delivery of oracles from God. Apocalyptic literature, on the other hand, made partial use of these prophetic oracles while placing greater emphasis on a coded form of Israelite tradition and history.

TALES OF THE YOUNG MEN

Following their capture by the Babylonian king Nebuchadnezzar, Daniel and his friends are given Babylonian names: Belteshazzar, Shadrach, Meshach, and Abednego. This is only the first step in the policy of **acculturating** these young men into Babylonian culture. The aim is to seduce them into the affluent lifestyle of their captors, making them more loyal and sympathetic officials when they are sent back to Judah to serve as administrators. This was a policy used by many of the empires in the ancient

Near East (see Neh 2:1–9). The assumption was that conquered peoples would be less likely to revolt if their own people administered them. And by bringing certain individuals at an early age to the capital of the empire and educating them alongside the sons of Babylonian nobles and officials, the Babylonians could ensure the loyalty of these local officials. The irony in these stories is that Daniel and his friends refuse to be "educated."

These tales have two different types of plots. First are the tests of courage. In these stories, Daniel and his friends stand as heroic role models for the oppressed exiles (Dan 1, 3, 5). Since this material was most likely composed during the Hellenistic era, the danger of cultural extinction faced by the youths in these stories may exemplify the conditions faced by the Jews under the influence of Seleucid Greeks, who ruled Syria-Palestine during the first half of the second century B.C.E.

The second plot type centers on Daniel's ability to interpret the visions and dreams of the Babylonian and Persian rulers (Dan 2, 4, 6). Like Joseph in Gen 41, Daniel shows greater wisdom and skill as a diviner than anyone in the court of the king of Babylon. Also like Joseph, Daniel claims that his powers come from God alone.

Stories of Heroic Fortitude and Wisdom

Dietary Laws Upheld. The Jewish trainees are given the privilege of eating from the king's table. In other biblical stories, this privilege is a sign of membership in the ruler's official family (1 Sam 20–29; 2 Sam 9:7–13). But since these foods would not have been prepared according to the dietary laws of the Jews (Lev 17:10–16; 20:25) and might also contain forbidden items (Lev 11:1–47; Deut 14:3–21), Daniel and his friends refuse to eat them. Instead they ask to be tested for ten days, during which they would consume only water and vegetables while other persons eat the king's rich food (Dan 1:8–14). At the conclusion of the test, the healthier diet of Daniel and company is demonstrated, and they are rewarded by God with wisdom and insight (1:15–17; compare Solomon's gift of wisdom in 1 Kgs 3:10–12). Here and in the other stories as well, Nebuchadnezzar rewards the men with positions of importance

(Dan 1:18–20; 2:48–49; compare Gen 41:37–45). The courage and intelligence shown by Daniel and his friends would have been a very useful model of behavior for the people enduring the oppression of the Seleucid king Antiochus IV (1 Macc 1:10–64), which led to the Maccabean revolt (168–142 B.C.E.).

Idolatry Refused. Shadrach, Meshach, and Abednego refuse to bow down and worship an idol as Nebuchadnezzar has commanded (Dan 3:1–12; compare 1 Macc 2:15–28). Their punishment is to be thrown into a furnace, possibly a huge brick kiln, and consumed by the flames (Dan 3:13–23). Miraculously, they survive with the aid of an angelic being (3:25–26). The story allows for the development of the theme of **universalism,** as Nebuchadnezzar declares his faith in the "God of Shadrach, Meshach, and Abednego" (3:28–30; compare 2 Kgs 5:15–19 and Dan 2:46–47). The refusal to worship an idol, of course, shows strict adherence to the prohibition of images (Exod 20:4–6), but it is also remarkably similar to the story of the martyrdom of Eleazar, who also refused to go "over to an alien nation" during Antiochus Epiphanes' oppression (2 Macc 6:18–31).

Daily Prayer Upheld. In an episode very similar to the harrowing escape in Dan 3, Daniel is placed in a den of hungry lions for disobeying the king's decree and praying to Yahweh (6:13–17). Once again divine intervention saves the life of the faithful person (6:19–22), and there is even a comic twist when the king, who had been tricked into sentencing Daniel to death, orders his unfaithful advisers to be cast into the lions' den (6:24; compare Esth 7:5–10).

Stories of Daniel as Diviner and Champion of Yahweh   In Dan 2, 4, and 5, Daniel exercises his ability to interpret dreams and signs. Each story demonstrates the insight given to this *hakam,* wise man, which far exceeds that of the king or any of his advisers (compare Gen 41:1–45). In the first story, Nebuchadnezzar has had a troubling dream of a mighty statue, divided into four separate sections of different metals (Dan 2:31–35), which is destroyed by a stone thrown from heaven. Daniel's interpretation identifies the four different metals in the statue as representing the successive kingdoms that have conquered and ruled Israel and/or Judah. The statue's destruction marks Yahweh's intervention in history and heralds the establishment of an eternal kingdom (2:36-45). Nebuchadnezzar is greatly impressed, promotes Daniel, and praises the power of his God, a clear example of the universalism theme (2:47-49).

Nebuchadnezzar's second troubling dream begins and ends much like the first. He sees a bounteous tree that, like the statue, is ordered destroyed by the "decree of the Most High" (4:10-17). Daniel identifies the tree as Nebuchadnezzar himself, and he tells him that the king has brought great blessings to his people just as the tree has nurtured the creatures that inhabited its branches. Because Nebuchadnezzar has failed to recognize Yahweh's power, however, he is doomed to be humbled by a period of insanity, after which he will freely acknowledge the power of Yahweh above all else (4:24-37).

The story of Belshazzar's feast in Dan 5 is the last example of Daniel's interpretative ability. Belshazzar, coregent in Babylon with his father, Nabonidus, pridefully stages a feast and serves his guests from the sacred vessels that have been taken from the Jerusalem temple. In response, a hand materializes and writes a series of Aramaic words on the wall of the banquet hall: "Mene, Mene, Tekel, and Parsin" (5:2-9). At his queen's urging, Belshazzar summons Daniel to interpret the meaning of these words. Daniel predicts the destruction of a kingdom whose days have been numbered *(mene)*, whose sins have been weighed on the scales *(tekel)*, and that will be "divided *[parsin]* and given to the Medes and Persians" (5:25-28). This story differs from the other two because it does not result either in Belshazzar's praising Yahweh or in Daniel's personal advancement. Daniel's stature as a true seer is proven, however, when the predicted events occur (5:30; compare Gen 41:46-57).

APOCALYPTIC VISIONS

The apocalyptic visions in Daniel can be treated more as a whole than the earlier tales. They share the common **eschatological** theme that the present age is evil. All good things have been subverted, and evil seems to be winning everywhere. The righteous are being oppressed and need encouragement to continue in their faith. One ancient Egyptian text, the "Visions of Neferti," describes the disintegration of Egyptian society prior to the breakup of the Old Kingdom (1991–1786 B.C.E.) and contains the same gloomy appraisal of a world gone mad. This Egyptian sage sees Egypt "in chaos," a land where "no order prevails" and in which "no one sheds a tear for Egypt" (*OTP*, pp. 313–15).

Characteristics of Apocalyptic Literature

Primary Characteristics

1. Dualism (a universe constantly divided between the forces of good/light and evil/darkness).

2. Eschatology (emphasis on "final days").

Secondary Characteristics

1. Visions interpreted by angelic being.

2. Animal symbolism (often a bizarre mixture of images).

3. Numerology (significant numbers assigned to forecast events or enumerate past events).

4. Angelic and demonic armies in perpetual struggle.

In the face of such disaster, the climactic intervention of God is the last hope of the righteous, since this age cannot be expected to survive. Just as in Zechariah's frightening apocalyptic vision (Zech 14:1–5), great persecution, turbulence, and warfare must precede the end. The more intense the conflict, the more evident it is to the righteous that the end of the age is approaching.

This understanding of the end of the world, as well as the use of angels as leaders of Yahweh's forces, may have been influenced, or at least reinforced, by Zoroastrianism, the dualistic Persian religion practiced during this period. The apocalyptic visions in Daniel contain many similarities to Zoroastrianism, and it can be said that Judaism underwent some marked changes during the Persian and Hellenistic periods. These include the addition, among at least a segment of the population, of a concept of resurrection. This concept is clearly reflected in Dan 12:2: "Many of those who sleep in the dust of the earth shall awake, some to everlasting life, and some to shame and everlasting contempt." And according to the Jewish historian Josephus, many Pharisees adopted this belief (*Jewish Antiquities* 18.14–15).

SUMMARY OF THE VISIONS

The visions in Dan 7–12 are filled with conflict on earth and among the angel armies of Yahweh and Persia. They end with the eventual downfall of the kingdoms that have oppressed Israel and the emergence of Yahweh as the supreme God (compare Mal 4:1–5). Daniel 7 contains a vision of deliverance from an oppression that is symbolized by four fantastic beasts: a lion with eagle's wings, a bear with three tusks, a leopard with four wings and four heads, and a beast too terrible to describe, with iron teeth and ten horns (7:3–8). Like the multilayered statue in Dan 2, each beast represents a kingdom that has oppressed Judah and Israel, and the various wings, heads, and horns represent the individual kings of these empires. The consensus among scholars today is that the beasts represent, in this order, Babylon (Chaldean), Medes, Persians, and Seleucids. Finally, the Seleucid king Antiochus IV is the small horn who plucks out three others in the fourth beast (7:8, 23–25).

The reign of these kingdoms ends with the decree of the enthroned "Ancient One," who appoints a **messiah**-like figure to exercise everlasting dominion over all peoples and nations (7:9–14). One of the angelic attendants explains to Daniel that the fourth beast was the last to oppress Israel (7:23–28). The reference to the attempt "to change the sacred seasons and the law" may well be a reference to Antiochus Epiphanes' attempt to suppress Jewish worship (1 Macc 1:44–50).

The vision in Dan 8 expresses a similar outcome for the reigning kingdoms. This vision depicts the warring of a ram, which represents the Medes/Persians, and a he-goat, which represents the successors of Alexander. The vision also introduces the angelic interpreter Gabriel, who softens the terrifying experience for Daniel (8:15–17). Once again an agent of God, the "Prince of Princes" (8:23–25), will extinguish the destructive efforts of the evil leaders. Daniel 9 reveals, however, that evil and oppression will last for "seventy weeks of years" (490 years); this odd expression reflects an interpretation of Jeremiah's prophecy of a seventy-year exile (Jer 25:11–12; 29:10), an interpretation that seeks to apply that prophecy to the events of the mid–second century B.C.E.

In the vision of Dan 10–12, Daniel learns more about the last days from the angel Michael (10:13–14). The vision contains a series of episodes, each prefaced with the statement "In those times" or "At the time of the end" (11:7, 14, 20, 29, 40). The episodes describe the Seleucid period from the writer's own day into the immediate future and are filled with descriptions of the disorder caused by uprising and the overthrow of Seleucid kings (11:2–45). In Dan 12, Daniel is assured that despite the long periods of conflict, evil, and disorder, God will ultimately deliver those who remain faithful (compare Joel 2:30–32):

> At that time Michael, the great prince, the protector of your people shall arise. There shall be a time of anguish, such as has never occurred since nations first came into existence. But at that time your people shall be delivered, everyone who is found written in the book. (Dan 12:1)

In addition, the righteous can expect a reward beyond this life:

> Happy are those who persevere and attain the 1,335 days. But you, go your way, and rest; you shall rise for your reward at the end of the days. (12:12–13)

These statements encourage the Jews to remain faithful to their ancestral religion despite political oppression and the allure of Hellenistic culture. They demonstrate the superiority of Yahweh, who is in control of everything, including the events of history and the gods of the other nations. This **theodicy** thus explains how the Jews can continue to face oppression without succumbing to cultural extinction. It also demonstrates the ways in which Judaism evolved out of the original Mesopotamian and Canaanite beliefs that formed much of the early fabric of Israelite worship into a strictly monotheistic religion.

GLOSSARY

A note on glossary items: The first occurrence in a chapter of the following words is bold.

acculturation: the submergence of a people and their culture into the culture of another people through close contact.

annunciation: a birth announcement.

anthropomorphic: giving a god human characteristics.

apocalyptic: a type of literature dealing with "end things" and characterized by verbal or numerical symbols, monstrous visions, and predictions of final battles.

apology: a literary device used to defend an individual.

apostasy: any action that allows or condones false worship.

archaeology: the scientific process of examining the ancient remains of human settlements and the artifacts produced by these people.

ark of the covenant: the gold-covered box created to house the Ten Commandments. It was carried by the Levites and was kept in the holy of holies of the tabernacle during the wilderness period.

artifact: anything that human beings have modified. In an archaeological excavation, artifacts are objects found within each stratum or occupation layer that are used to clarify and date the site.

Asherah pole: Asherah was the divine consort of the Canaanite god Baal. She was often represented by a sacred pole erected near an altar (Exod 34:13) or by a sacred grove of trees (Deut 16:21).

B.C.E.: "Before the Common Era"—used in this book in place of B.C., but the dates are the same.

call: the event when a person is called to become a prophet.

canon: the books designated by the faith community as holy Scripture and the standard for faith and practice.

casting his mantle: an action designed to designate someone as a person's successor.

C.E.: "Common Era"—used in this book in place of A.D., but the dates are the same.

Chronicler: this biblical editor is said to be responsible for the books of 1 and 2 Chronicles and possibly Ezra and Nehemiah. The work most likely dates to the late fifth century B.C.E. It contains a revised history of Israel from the time of David until the postexilic period.

city-state: a political unit comprising an urban center and its immediate environs and villages.

cognitive dissonance: a situation in which two completely credible statements are made, one of which is necessarily false.

colophon: a statement or phrase placed at the end of a document. The colophon may serve as a summary or simply an end marker.

corporate identity: a legal principle according to which an entire household is rewarded or punished for the righteousness or sins of the head of the household.

cosmopolitan: an attitude of cultural openness and sophistication.

covenant: the contractual agreement between Yahweh and the people, in which Yahweh promises land and children in exchange for the people's exclusive worship and obedience.

covenant renewal ceremony: a ritual used several times by Israelite leaders to reinforce the importance of the covenant with Yahweh.

cultic: anything having to do with religious activity.

Deuteronomist: the name given to the author/authors associated with the book of Deuteronomy (the D-source in the Documentary Hypothesis) and a layer of editing in Joshua–2 Kings. Dated to ca. 600 B.C.E., this source reflects a strict moralism and a view of Israelite history in which the people continually fail to obey the covenant and therefore deserve Yahweh's punishment.

Diaspora Judaism: the conservative strand of Judaism that evolved during the exile and is characteristic of the Jews who remained in the lands of the exile.

divination: a set of practices that attempt to determine the future and the will of the gods. These practices include casting lots, examining animal entrails, and seeking patterns in natural phenomena.

Divine Assembly: the divine company that serves Yahweh in the form of messengers and is portrayed surrounding Yahweh enthroned.

Divine Warrior: the role of Yahweh in warfare.

egalitarian: Denoting a social system in which all persons have equal status.

enacted prophecy: a prophecy that uses an action by the prophet to draw attention and reinforce the message.

endogamy: a policy of marrying only within a certain identifiable group.

Ephraim: son of Joseph and the generic political name synonymous with the northern kingdom of Israel.

eschatology: the study of "last things," or events just prior to the end of time.

etiological: regarding a story that explains the origin of a event, the background of a place-name, or the basis for a tradition.

execration ritual: a set of actions that curse a person or place.

framework story: a narrative that, when analyzed, shows an outline structure that can be applied whenever a similar set of events occur or can be used as the basis for a drama.

genre: a category of literature (e.g., short story, poetry).

hegemony: a political situation in which a powerful nation or empire exercises extensive influence over the policies and actions of neighboring states.

herem: holy war in which all captured property and persons are destroyed as a dedicatory sacrifice to God (see the conquest of Jericho in Josh 6).

hesed: "everlasting love"—a covenantal term and the basis for Yahweh's willingness to make a covenant with the people.

high place: known in Hebrew as *bamah*, the high place is a nearby hill or local shrine that served both the needs of the village culture as well as cities such as Dan. Although Yahweh was worshiped at the high place, other gods were also worshiped here. They were banned by the kings of Judah, but continued in use in Israel through their history (part of the "sins of Jeroboam" in 1 Kgs 12:25-33).

lament: a genre, found principally in the Psalms and the book of Lamentations, that expresses the sorrow or suffering of an individual or a group.

liturgy: the outline and stages of a worship service.

messiah: from the Hebrew word *mashiyah*, "anointed," used for individuals chosen by Yahweh for leadership positions.

motif: a repeated idea or theme in a narrative.

myth: a story that centers on the origin of events or things (see etiological) and usually involves the activities of gods.

oracle: a prophetic speech.

oracles against the nations: this particular type of prophetic speech is designed to pronounce judgment on Israel's neighbors. For example, Ezek 25-29 contains a series of proclamations against various countries, including Ammon, Tyre (Phoenicia), and Egypt.

Pentateuch: the first five books of the Old Testament/Hebrew Bible, Genesis through Deuteronomy.

prophetic immunity: protection given to prophets when they speak in a god's name and preventing the people from killing the messenger because of a negative message.

proselytes: converts to a faith community.

remnant: the portion of the community who will, according to the prophets, survive God's wrath and rebuild the nation.

ritual purity: the steps taken to transform persons or objects into a "clean" or "pure" religious state.

Sabbath: the celebration of Yahweh as the creator God and the commemoration of the creation event by ceasing work one day each week.

sackcloth: a roughly woven garment worn as a sign of mourning or repentance.

Septuagint: the Greek translation of the Hebrew Bible by the Alexandrian (Egypt) Jews from the fourth to second century B.C.E.; it is abbreviated LXX and contains the Apocrypha, or Deuterocanonical books of the Bible.

seventy elders: the group of men selected to help administer the Israelites and representing them at major events.

sins of Jeroboam: the actions taken by King Jeroboam I to establish a separate identity for the northern kingdom. These sins become the hallmark of an "evil king."

sons of the prophet: apprentice prophets who serve Elijah and Elisha as a support group and as messengers.

superscription: an instruction containing information on orchestration, instrumentation, and melody, placed before the first verse of a psalm.

syncretism: the borrowing of cultural ideas and traits from neighboring peoples.

theodicy: an explanation for God's actions; most often found in the words of the prophets.

theophany: the appearance of God to a human being.

transcendent: of a deity—separate from the creation and not affected by the forces of nature.

treaty: a formal agreement that defines the relationship between two nations or peoples.

universalism: in the biblical narrative, a theme that attempts to demonstrate that Yahweh is a universal god by having a non-Israelite make a statement of faith or remark about Yahweh's power.

Via Maris: the name of an international highway that extended at least from Upper Galilee to the Mediterranean coast of Palestine by way of the Jezreel Valley. It may have also extended south along the coast to Egypt and north to Damascus.

wisdom (literature): a type of literature that concentrates on the basic values and common sense of a culture.

Yahweh: one of the names for the Israelite God in the Bible. Sometimes anglicized into Jehovah, it is associated with the J-source in the Pentateuch, according to the Documentary Hypothesis. In the English translation of the Bible, Yahweh is often translated LORD.

SELECT BIBLIOGRAPHY

A NOTE ON SOURCES

I have relied on the work of many other scholars in writing this survey of the Hebrew prophets. However, I have chosen to provide only a select bibliography. General works and the major commentaries written on individual prophets' books dominate this list so that students may come to recognize the principal works in the field. The literature on ancient Near Eastern and biblical prophecy is quite rich, and any bibliography will be out-of-date as soon as it is published. As a result, I have created several on-line bibliographies to assist students; since they are continually being updated, they provide a more vibrant source for further reading on the prophets:

http://courses.smsu.edu/vhm970f/bib/PROPHET.html—a general bibliography for Hebrew prophets

http://courses.smsu.edu/vhm970f/bib/ISAIAH-02.html—a select bibliography for Isaiah

http://courses.smsu.edu/vhm970f/bib/JERBIB-02.html—a select bibliography for Jeremiah

GENERAL REFERENCE

The Anchor Bible Dictionary. Edited by D. N. Freedman. 5 vols. New York: Doubleday, 1992.

Ancient Near Eastern Texts. Edited by James Pritchard. Princeton: Princeton University Press,1969.

The Cambridge Ancient History. Edited by J. Boardman et al. Cambridge: Cambridge University Press, 1970–.

Civilizations of the Ancient Near East. Edited by Jack Sasson. 4 vols. New York: Scribners, 1995. Repr. 4 vols in 2. Peabody, Mass.: Hendrickson, 2001.

Context of Scripture. Edited by W. W. Hallo and K. L. Younger. Leiden: E. J. Brill, 1997.

Dictionary of Biblical Imagery. Edited by L. Ryken et al. Downers Grove, Ill.: InterVarsity, 1998.

Dictionary of Deities and Demons in the Bible. Edited by K. van der Toorn et al. Leiden: E. J. Brill, 1995.

The New Encyclopedia of Archaeological Excavations in the Holy Land. Edited by E. Stern. New York: Simon & Schuster, 1993.

The Oxford Encyclopedia of Archaeology in the Near East. Edited by E. Meyers. 5 vols. New York: Oxford University Press, 1997.

BOOKS ON PARTICULAR ASPECTS OF BIBLE BACKGROUND

Beitzel, B. *The Moody Atlas of Bible Lands.* Chicago: Moody, 1985.

Berquist, J. *Judaism in Persia's Shadow.* Minneapolis: Fortress, 1995.

Blenkinsopp, J. *Sage, Priest, Prophet: Religious and Intellectual Leadership in Ancient Israel.* Louisville: Westminster John Knox, 1995.

Borowski, O. *Agriculture in Iron Age Israel.* Winona Lake, Ind.: Eisenbrauns, 1987.

———. *Every Living Thing.* Walnut Creek, Cal.: Alta Mira, 1998.

Bottéro, J. *Mesopotamia.* Chicago: University of Chicago Press, 1992.

Cook, S. L. *Prophecy and Apocalypticism: The Postexilic Social Setting.* Minneapolis: Fortress, 1995.

Cross, F. M. *Canaanite Myth and Hebrew Epic.* Cambridge: Harvard University Press, 1971.

Cryer, F. H. *Divination in Ancient Israel and Its Near Eastern Environment.* Sheffield, England: JSOTS, 1994.

Davies, W. D., et al. *The Persian Period.* Vol. 1 of *The Cambridge History of Judaism.* Cambridge: Cambridge University Press, 1984.

Dearman, A. *Religion and Culture in Ancient Israel.* Peabody, Mass.: Hendrickson, 1992.

Dempsey, C. J. *The Prophets: A Liberation-Critical Reading.* Minneapolis: Fortress, 2000.

Eshkenazi, T., and K. Richards, eds. *Second Temple Studies.* Journal for the Study of the Old Testament, Supplement Series, 175. Sheffield: Sheffield Academic, 1994.

Gershevitch, I., ed. *The Median and Achaemenid Periods.* Vol. 2 of *The Cambridge History of Iran.* Cambridge: Cambridge University Press, 1985.

Gowan, D. E. *Theology of the Prophetic Books: The Death and Resurrection of Israel.* Louisville: Westminster John Knox, 1998.

Grabbe, L. *Judaism from Cyrus to Hadrian.* Minneapolis: Fortress, 1992.

————. *Priests, Prophets, Diviners, Sages: A Socio-historical Study of Religious Specialists in Ancient Israel.* Valley Forge, Pa.: Trinity International, 1995.

Hoerth, A., G. Mattingly, and E. Yamauchi. *Peoples of the Old Testament World.* Grand Rapids, Mich.: Baker, 1994.

Horowitz, W. *Mesopotamian Cosmic Geography.* Winona Lake, Ind.: Eisenbrauns, 1998.

Jacobsen, T. *Treasures of Darkness.* New Haven: Yale University Press, 1976.

————. *The Harps That Once.* New Haven: Yale University Press, 1987.

Keel, O. *The Symbolism of the Biblical World.* New York: Seabury, 1978.

Keel, O., and C. Uehlinger. *Gods, Goddesses, and Images of God in Ancient Israel.* Minneapolis: Fortress, 1998.

King, P. *Hosea, Amos, Hosea, Micah: An Archaeological Commentary.* Philadelphia: Westminster John Knox, 1988.

Kuhrt, A. *The Ancient Near East, 3000–330 BC*. London: Routledge, 1997.

Lambert, W. G. *Babylonian Wisdom Literature*. Oxford: Clarendon Press, 1960.

Lichtheim, Miriam. *Ancient Egyptian Literature*. Berkeley: University of California Press, 1980.

Matthews, V. H. *Manners and Customs in the Bible*. Peabody, Mass.: Hendrickson, 1988.

Matthews, V. H., and D. C. Benjamin. *The Social World of Ancient Israel*. Peabody, Mass: Hendrickson, 1993.

Mazar, Amihai. *Archaeology of the Land of the Bible*. New York: Doubleday, 1990.

Miller, J. M., and J. Hayes. *A History of Ancient Israel and Judah*. Philadelphia: Westminster John Knox, 1986.

Nemet-Nejat, Karen Rhea. *Daily Life in Ancient Mesopotamia*. Westport, Conn.: Greenwood, 1998.

Overholt, T. W. *Channels of Prophecy: The Social Dynamics of Prophetic Activity*. Minneapolis: Fortress, 1989.

Peckham, B. *History and Prophecy: The Development of Late Judean Literary Traditions*. New York: Doubleday, 1993.

Pleins, J. D. *The Social Visions of the Hebrew Bible*. Louisville: Westminster John Knox, 2001.

Rasmussen, Carl. *NIV Atlas of the Bible*. Grand Rapids, Mich.: Zondervan, 1989.

Redford, D. B. *Egypt, Canaan, and Israel in Ancient Times*. Princeton: Princeton University Press, 1992.

Reiner, E. *Astral Magic in Babylonia*. Philadelphia: American Philosophical Society, 1995.

Roaf, M. *Cultural Atlas of Mesopotamia and the Ancient Near East*. New York: Facts-on-File, 1990.

Saggs, H. W. F. *The Greatness That Was Babylon*. New York: Mentor, 1962.

———. *Encounter with the Divine in Mesopotamia and Israel*. London: Athlone, 1978.

———. *The Might That Was Assyria*. London: Sidgwick & Jackson, 1984.

Snell, D. *Life in the Ancient Near East*. New Haven: Yale University Press, 1997.

Toorn, K. van der. *Sin and Sanction in Israel and Mesopotamia.* Assen, Netherlands: Van Gorcum, 1985.

Weinfeld, M. *Social Justice in Ancient Israel.* Minneapolis: Fortress, 1995.

Wiseman, D. J. *Nebuchadrezzar and Babylon.* New York: Oxford University Press, 1985.

Wright, C. J. H. *God's People in God's Land.* Grand Rapids, Mich.: Eerdmans, 1990.

Yamauchi, E. *Persia and the Bible.* Grand Rapids, Mich.: Baker, 1990.

COMMENTARIES

Isaiah

Oswalt, J. *The Book of Isaiah.* 2 vols. Grand Rapids, Mich.: Eerdmans, 1986–1997.

Watts, J. D. W. *Isaiah 1–33.* Waco, Tex.: Word, 1985.

———. *Isaiah 34–66.* Waco, Tex.: Word, 1987.

Wildberger, H. *Isaiah 1–12.* Minneapolis: Fortress, 1991.

———. *Isaiah 13–27.* Minneapolis: Fortress, 1998.

Jeremiah

Holladay, W. *Jeremiah 1.* Minneapolis: Fortress, 1986.

———. *Jeremiah 2.* Minneapolis: Fortress, 1989.

Keown, G. L., P. J. Scalise, and T. G. Smothers. *Jeremiah 26–52.* Dallas: Word, 1995.

Thompson, J. A. *The Book of Jeremiah.* Grand Rapids, Mich.: Eerdmans, 1980.

Ezekiel

Allen, L. *Ezekiel.* 2 vols. Dallas: Word, 1990–1994.

Block, D. I. *The Book of Ezekiel.* 2 vols. Grand Rapids, Mich.: Eerdmans, 1997–1998.

Bodi, D. *The Book of Ezekiel and the Poem of Erra.* Freiburg, Switzer-
    land: Vandenhoeck & Ruprecht, 1991.
Greenberg, M. *Ezekiel 1–20.* New York: Doubleday, 1983.
———. *Ezekiel 21–37.* New York: Doubleday, 1997.
Zimmerli, W. *Ezekiel 1.* Minneapolis: Fortress, 1979.
———. *Ezekiel 2.* Minneapolis: Fortress, 1983.

Daniel

Baldwin, J. *Daniel.* Downers Grove, Ill.: InterVarsity, 1978.
Collins, J. J. *Daniel.* Minneapolis: Fortress, 1993.
Goldingay, J. *Daniel.* Dallas: Word, 1989.

Hosea

Andersen, F. I., and D. N. Freedman. *Hosea.* New York: Doubleday,
    1980.
MacIntosh, A. A. *A Critical and Exegetical Commentary on Hosea.*
    Edinburgh: T&T Clark, 1997.
Stuart, D. *Hosea–Jonah.* Dallas: Word, 1987.
Wolff, H. W. *A Commentary on the Book of the Prophet Hosea.* Minne-
    apolis: Fortress, 1974.

Joel

Allen, L. *The Books of Joel, Obadiah, Jonah, and Micah.* Grand Rapids,
    Mich.: Eerdmans, 1976.
Crenshaw, J. *Joel.* New York: Doubleday, 1995.
Hubbard, D. *Joel, Amos.* Downers Grove, Ind.: InterVarsity, 1989.
Stuart, D. *Hosea–Jonah.* Dallas: Word, 1987.
Wolff, H. W. *Joel and Amos.* Minneapolis: Fortress, 1977.

Amos

Andersen, F. I., and D. N. Freedman. *Amos.* New York: Doubleday,
    1989.
Jeremias, J. *The Book of Amos.* Louisville, Ky.: Westminster John
    Knox, 1998.
Paul, S. *A Commentary on the Book of Amos.* Minneapolis: Fortress,
    1991.

Wolff, H. W. *A Commentary on the Books of the Prophets Joel and Amos*. Minneapolis: Fortress, 1977.

Obadiah

Allen, L. C. *The Books of Joel, Obadiah, Jonah, and Micah*. Grand Rapids, Mich.: Eerdmans, 1976.
Raabe, P. R. *Obadiah*. New York: Doubleday, 1996.
Wolff, H. W. *Obadiah and Jonah*. Minneapolis: Fortress, 1986.

Jonah

Limburg, J. *Jonah*. Louisville: Westminster John Knox, 1993.
Sasson, J. *Jonah*. New York: Doubleday, 1990.
Walton, J. *Jonah*. Grand Rapids, Mich.: Zondervan, 1982.
Wolff, H. W. *Obadiah and Jonah*. Minneapolis: Fortress, 1986.

Micah

Ben Zvi, E. *Micah*. Grand Rapids, Mich.: Eerdmans, 2000.
Hillers, D. *Micah*. Minneapolis: Fortress, 1983.
Mays, J. M. *Micah*. Philadelphia: Westminster, 1976.

Nahum

Baker, D. *Nahum, Habakkuk, Zephaniah*. Downers Grove, Ill.: InterVarsity, 1988.
Roberts, J. J. M. *Nahum, Habakkuk, and Zephaniah: A Commentary*. Louisville: Westminster John Knox, 1991.

Habakkuk

Roberts, J. J. M. *Nahum, Habakkuk, and Zephaniah: A Commentary*. Louisville: Westminster John Knox, 1991.
Smith, R. L. *Micah–Malachi*. Waco, Tex.: Word, 1984.

Zephaniah

Berlin, A. *Zephaniah*. New York: Doubleday, 1994.
Roberts, J. J. M. *Nahum, Habakkuk, and Zephaniah: A Commentary*. Louisville: Westminster John Knox, 1991.
Smith, R. L. *Micah–Malachi*. Waco, Tex.: Word, 1984.

Haggai

Meyers, E., and C. Meyers. *Haggai and Zechariah 1–8*. New York: Doubleday, 1987.

Verhoef, P. A. *The Books of Haggai and Malachi*. Grand Rapids, Mich.: Eerdmans, 1986.

Wolff, H. W. *Haggai*. Minneapolis: Fortress, 1988.

Zechariah

Ellis, R. S. *Foundation Deposits in Ancient Mesopotamia*. New Haven: Yale University Press, 1968.

Halpern, B. "The Ritual Background of Zechariah's Temple Song." *Catholic Biblical Quarterly* 40 (1978): 167–190.

Meyers, E., and C. Meyers. *Zechariah 9–14*. New York: Doubleday, 1993.

Malachi

Glazier-McDonald, B. *The Divine Messenger*. Atlanta: Scholars Press, 1987.

Hill, A. *Malachi*. New York: Doubleday, 1998.

Petersen, D. L. *Zechariah 9–14 and Malachi*. Louisville: Westminster John Knox, 1995.

INDEX OF NAMES AND SUBJECTS

Index of Ancient Sources